Routledge Introductions to Development

Series Editors:
John Bale and David Drakakis-Smith

An Introduction to Sustainable Development

'Development which meets the needs of the present without compromising the ability of future generations to meet their own needs.'

As the Brundtland Commission's definition suggests, sustainable development faces challenges from the interdependence of peoples and places throughout the globe. While environmental concerns threaten the 'quality of life', the 'pollution of poverty' may threaten life itself. Sustainable development encapsulates the realisation that to achieve the goals of either conservation or development, the welfare needs of the poorest groups must be addressed.

Sustainable Development identifies how and why future development patterns and processes must be sustainable on a global scale. From an examination of the historical origins of the concept, the text explores the current patterns and future challenges of resource use in rural and urban environments. Synthesising material from a diversity of more specialised volumes, and from developing nations at a variety of spatial scales, this introductory text will prove an invaluable source for students of Geography, Sociology, Development and Environmental Studies in both developed and developing countries.

A volume in the **Routledge Introductions to Development** series edited by John Bale and David Drakakis-Smith.

In the same series

Jennifer A. Elliott

An Introduction to Sustainable Development

The developing world

London and New York

First published 1994
by Routledge
11 New Fetter Lane, London EC4P 4EE

Simultaneously published in the USA and Canada
by Routledge
29 West 35th Street, New York, NY 10001

Typeset in Times by J&L Composition Ltd, Filey, North Yorkshire
Printed and bound in Great Britain by Biddles Ltd, Guildford and King's Lynn

British Library Cataloguing in Publication Data
A catalogue record for this book is available from the British Library

Library of Congress Cataloging in Publication Data
Elliott, Jennifer A.
    An Introduction to Sustainable Development : The Developing World /
Jennifer A. Elliott.
        p.   cm. – (Routledge introductions to development)
    Includes bibliographical references and index.
    1. Sustainable development – Developing countries.
2. Environmental policy – Developing countries.   I. Title.
II. Series.
HC59.72.E5E43   1994
338.9′009172′4 – dc20   93–17692

ISBN 0–415–06954–8

To my parents, Ian and Sally Elliott

Contents

Plates

Figures

Tables

Acknowledgements

I should like to thank Garry Power for motivating me to write this book. I am grateful also to many colleagues and students for their comments and advice given during the process of compiling the material. In particular, Gordon Walker and Stephen W. Williams at Staffordshire University who gave very valuable assistance often at short notice and Sioux Cumming of the University of Zimbabwe who produced many of the diagrams. Similarly, I would like to thank the Editors of this series for their time and direction.

Finally, there are many family members and friends to whom I am grateful for their continued support, flexibility and humour.

1
What is sustainable development?

Introduction

This book is concerned with the problem of finding sustainable patterns and processes of development within the international community for the future. In the developing world, conditions such as rising poverty and mounting debt form the context in which individuals struggle to meet their basic needs of survival and nations wrestle to provide for their populations. The outcome is often the destruction of the very resources with which such needs will have to be met in the future. In the developed world, there is a rising awareness of the environmental effects and the wasteful use of resources associated with their own style of development. It is recognized that these patterns and processes of development will not be able to continue to supply the needs of a minority of the world's population let alone the rising numbers of people who aspire to higher standards of living.

One of the primary aims of the book is to highlight the progress made to date towards establishing new patterns and processes of development which are sustainable. Understanding the characteristics of successful sustainable development projects will be essential for meeting the ongoing challenge of balancing present needs against those of the future. It will be seen that the prospects of sustainable development in any one location are in part shaped by forces and decision-making often at great distances away. It is therefore impossible to consider the developing world in isolation from the wider global community. However, the major focus of this book is on the factors influencing sustainable development in the developing world.

In the book, the challenges and opportunities of sustainable development will be seen to lie in both the natural and the human environment. For example, many countries of what can be termed the developing world are in the tropics. The tropical ecosystem is a fragile environment and is easily disturbed (see Gupta in this series). Large sections of the populations of these countries live in physical environments in which securing basic needs is extremely problematic and which may even be detrimental to human health. Often, people contribute to the further degradation of already poor environments in the course of trying to meet their survival requirements. However, as the environment deteriorates, so do standards of living and the prospects for meeting future needs. Characteristics of the human environment of the developing world include rapid population growth, rising numbers of people in absolute poverty, increasing urbanization, widespread ill health, high levels of unemployment and a lack of skilled personnel. These are just some of the characteristics of the natural and human environments of the developing world which ensure that the challenges of and opportunities for sustainable development are quite different from those of the developed countries.

However, the chapters of this book show that the challenge of sustainable development is not different for the developing and developed countries. In order to understand the characteristics of resource use or human condition in the developing world, it is essential to identify the underlying processes. Such processes operate at a variety of spatial scales from local (including the household) through to the global level. They include a large number of both physical and human processes. At all scales, it is these factors in combination which shape the relationships between people and the environment and also between people in different places. For example, a farmer anywhere in the world will decide what cash crops to grow not only on the basis of local soil characteristics (the natural environment) but also according to the price which can be expected for different crops (set by many factors including international levels of supply and demand).

It is through an understanding not only of the patterns of development and underdevelopment but also of the processes underlying these that the challenges and opportunities for sustainable development

Figure 1.1 Defining sustainable development

'Sustainable development: development that is likely to achieve lasting satisfaction of human needs and improvement of the quality of human life'
(Robert Allen, *How to Save the World*, London: Kogan Page, 1980).

'In broad terms the concept of sustainable development encompasses:

1 Help for the very poor because they are left with no option other than to destroy their environment;
2 The idea of self-reliant development, within natural resource constraints;
3 The idea of cost-effective development using differing economic criteria to the traditional approach; that is to say development should not degrade environmental quality, nor should it reduce productivity in the long run;
4 The great issues of health control, appropriate technologies, food self-reliance, clean water and shelter for all;
5 The notion that people-centred initiatives are needed; human beings, in other words, are the resources in the concept.'

(Mustafa Tolba, *Sustainable Development: Constraints and Opportunities*, London: Butterworth, 1987)

'The sustainable society is one that lives within the self-perpetuating limits of its environment. That society . . . is not a "no-growth" society. . . . It is, rather, a society that recognizes the limits of growth . . . and looks for alternative ways of growing'
(J. Coomer, *Quest for a Sustainable Society*, Oxford: Pergamon, 1979).

'The term "sustainable development" suggests that the lessons of ecology can, and should, be applied to economic processes'
(Michael Redclift, *Sustainable Development: Exploring the Contradictions*, London: Methuen, 1987).

'In principle, such an optimal (sustainable growth) policy would seek to maintain an "acceptable" rate of growth in per-capita real incomes without depleting the national capital asset stock or the natural environmental asset stock'
(R. K. Turner, *Sustainable Environmental Management*, London: Belhaven, 1988).

Source: Compiled from Pearce, D., Markandya, A. and Barbier, E. B. (1989) *Blueprint for a Green Economy*, London: Earthscan.

become clear. In the course of this book, it will be seen that sustainable development in the future requires actions for change at all levels, addressing both the human and physical environments and through interventions in physical, political-economic and social processes.

The concept of sustainable development

In 1984, the United Nations commissioned an independent group of twenty-two people from member states, drawn from both the developed and developing worlds, to identify long-term environmental strategies for the international community. In 1987, the World Commission on Environment and Development (WCED), also known as the Brundtland Commission, reported to the UN, calling for a 'common endeavour and for new norms of behaviour at all levels and in the interests of all'. Global cooperation and mutually supportive actions between countries at different stages of economic development were central themes within their report entitled *Our Common Future* (WCED 1987). Despite the extent of environmental decay which the Commission reported, they remained optimistic that, given global commitment and coordination, a more prosperous, more just and more secure future was possible for all.

Figure 1.2 Core issues and necessary conditions for sustainable development as identified by the World Commission on Environment and Development

Core issues:

- Population and development;
- Food security;
- Species and ecosystems;
- Energy;
- Industry;
- The urban challenge.

Pursuit of sustainable development requires:

- A political system that secures effective citizen participation in decision-making;
- An economic system that provides for solutions for the tensions arising from disharmonious development;
- A production system that respects the obligation to preserve the ecological base for development;
- A technological system that fosters sustainable patterns of trade and finance;
- An international system that fosters sustainable patterns of trade and finance;
- An administrative system that is flexible and has the capacity for self-correction.

Source: WCED (1987) *Our Common Future*, Oxford: Oxford University Press.

Although the WCED was not the first group to use the term 'sustainable development' (see Figure 1.1), they offered perhaps the most straightforward and certainly the most widely used definition. The WCED defined sustainable development as development which meets the needs of the present without compromising the ability of future generations to meet their own needs. However, the apparent simplicity of this definition was offset by the challenges that the Commission identified for effecting sustainable development in practice. Figure 1.2 highlights the core issues and necessary conditions for sustainable development in the future as identified by the WCED. The challenge of implementing sustainable development in practice is an ongoing one to which many governments, organizations and individuals have been addressing themselves throughout the 1980s and into the 1990s.

Adams (1990) has noted that 'the concept of sustainable development cannot be understood in a historical vacuum'. In order to identify the challenges of implementing sustainable development in practice and to realize the opportunities for sustainable development, it is necessary to understand the changes in thinking and practice from which the concept has developed. Of particular importance are the changes in thinking about what constitutes 'development' and how best to achieve it, and changing ideas about the 'environment'.

Changing perceptions of development

'Development' is something to which we all aspire and ideas about the best means of achieving our own aspirations and needs are potentially as old as human civilization. The study of development, however, has a much shorter history, really dating back only as far as the 1950s when colonial territories started to achieve independence. The first United Nations Development Decade of the 1960s was characterized by optimism and international cooperation. It was assumed that the development problems of the underdeveloped world would be solved quickly through the transfer of finance, technology and experience from the developed countries. The powering force behind development was thought to be economic growth, since it was argued that it had been economic growth which had taken the developed societies through to their own position.

However, in the light of rising world poverty and inequality in the 1970s (the second UN Development Decade), the optimism of such a speedy end to underdevelopment faded. Many developing countries had achieved economic growth as measured by Gross National Product (GNP) but this 'development' was not shared equally amongst the populations of these nations. For example, in Brazil in 1970, the poorest 40 per cent of the population received only 6.5 per cent of the total national income, in contrast to the 66.7 per cent of the total national income received by the richest 20 per cent of the population. In the 1970s, the international commitment to sharing and cooperation also declined. The recession of the early 1970s and the realization of the longer term nature of underdevelopment no doubt contributed to countries prioritizing their own development needs rather than those of others.

During the third UN Development Decade of the 1980s, international cooperation and, to a lesser extent, optimism re-emerged within the literature on development. A better understanding of development patterns across the globe and of the underlying processes which gave rise to those spatial patterns had highlighted the many ways in which the development prospects or achievements of all parts of the world were linked to each other. For example, people and places are linked interdependently, through issues such as trade, energy, employment and communications, within a world economy which reaches even the most remote communities. Distributional issues, such as improving the income levels of target populations, were now accepted as fundamental parts of any development strategy. 'Growth with Equity' or 'Redistribution with Growth' are phrases which emerged in the 1970s and encapsulate the recognition that fostering economic growth remains a fundamental ingredient within development thinking and action. However, the nature of economic growth is critical to ensuring that the benefits do not fall solely to a minority of the population.

'Development' in the 1980s was seen to be a multidimensional concept encapsulating widespread improvements in the social as well as the material well-being of all in society. In addition, it was recognized that there was no single model for achieving development and that investment in all sectors was required, including agriculture as well as industry. Above all, 'development' needed to be sustainable; it must encompass not only economic and social activities, but also those related to population, the use of natural resources and their resulting impacts on the environment. The multidimensional nature of the challenge of development is illustrated in case study A through the example of the interdependent nature of population and development concerns today.

Case study A

Interdependent goals: the case of population and development

During the 1960s, there was a concern in the developed world that the relatively high rates of population growth in the under-developed nations threatened to make the tasks of eliminating poverty, servicing the populations, creating employment and achieving development, extremely difficult. Neo-Malthusian ideas dominated this debate; in line with Malthus' original work, it was thought that population growth could not be matched by food production and the consequences of this would be seen in terms of starvation and premature deaths. In addition, because invest-ment had to be spread across greater and greater numbers, high population growth rates would have a negative effect on economic development. On the part of the developed world, therefore, the rapid rates of population growth were seen as the cause of underdevelopment in the developing world and curbing such growth was a necessary condition if these countries were to become developed.

This view dominated international thinking into the early 1970s and was a powerful force in promoting financial support for a whole host of programmes aimed at rapidly bringing down birth rates in the developing countries. High fertility in the under-developed nations was perceived to be a reflection of an unmet demand for contraception. The solution to development was therefore to provide these family planning services to the popula-tion such that they could control their own fertility and bring down growth rates; an apparently simple technical exercise of taking western contraceptive techniques and making them available in the developing world.

The strength of this school of thought was confirmed by the large amount of foreign aid which became available for such programmes. India was the first country to adopt a national family planning programme in 1951. Subsequently, expansion in the 1960s was most rapid in other parts of Asia and in Latin America; many African countries did not adopt such programmes until much later.

Case study A *(continued)*

Although these ideas have since been referred to as the 'condom school of thought', reflecting the importance attached to contraceptives in reducing population growth rates and enabling development to take place, condoms were rarely the central element of fertility control within such programmes. Often much more invasive methods were promoted, such as inter-uterine devices and even sterilization itself. It soon became clear that reducing fertility was not a simple technical exercise at all. For example, research into the uptake of family planning services in the early 1970s found that, when offered the services, the majority of women did not use them. Rather than high fertility resulting from an unmet demand for contraceptives, this suggested that family planning supply was actually outstripping demand. In addition, it was assumed that uptake of family planning techniques would simply diffuse outward from central project locations to neighbouring areas but, in fact, research found that there was no simple relationship between contraceptive use and distance from the project centre.

Many family planning programmes turned out in practice to be extremely unpopular and far from neutral exercises. In India, for example, it is accepted that public resentment to the mass sterilization programmes in the 1970s was a major factor in the defeat of Indira Gandhi's government in 1978. In the ten months from April 1976 to January 1977, seven million sterilizations were performed, but increased coercion, various malpractices and even forced sterilization of men with more than three children in some states meant that the campaign was far from a success. The 'technical' issue in theory had become a highly political and ethical one in practice. Throughout the campaigns, however, India's government was supported by the World Bank, western aid agencies and western governments, both in monetary terms and through statements praising the government's 'hardheadedness' in the family planning drive.

It was not only in India that re-evaluation of the role of family planning programmes was taking place in the 1970s. At the First World Population Conference in 1974, there was much disagreement between the developed and developing countries over the

Case study A *(continued)*

> relationship between population and development and the specific role of family planning programmes. However, by the Second World Population Conference in 1984, a more balanced view prevailed and the idea that development itself was the best form of contraception was widely held. It was acknowledged that the characteristics of underdevelopment, such as illiteracy, ill-health and lack of social services, were also those which were likely to impede fertility decline.
>
> Family planning programmes will have a continued role in the developing countries, since it is a basic human right to be able to choose the size of one's family. In addition, as traditional means of child spacing break down, there is a need for policies which increase knowledge of and access to modern means of contraception on the grounds of maternal and child health. However, these should be supported by a commitment to wider social planning.
>
> Population and development are now acknowledged to be interdependent goals; achievement with respect to either requires improvements in the other. It is thought that social change such as the decline in importance of the extended family may prove to have a much more important impact on fertility levels of developing countries than either economic development or the vigour of family planning or maternal or child health programmes.

Changing perceptions of the environment

The history of environmental concern is quite similar to that of development studies. Although people have held and articulated varying attitudes towards nature, stretching back many years, the 1960s have been identified as the period in which a coherent philosophy and language surrounding the environment was first formed. Since then, there have been significant changes in the way in which the environment has been viewed, in terms of both the people doing the viewing and the perceived conservation requirements.

In the 1960s, 'Environmentalism' as it was known was largely a movement reflecting European and American, white, middle-class concerns. Action groups, often supported by the media, campaigned on issues such as air pollution and whaling. The undesirable effects of industrial development were beginning to be seen and people were worried about the effects on their own lifestyles and health. In addition, these groups expressed concern regarding population expansion in the developing world and the threat that this posed to the environment through raising demands on a global resource base which was considered to be finite. Publications such as *The Population Bomb* by Ehrlich and *The Limits to Growth* by Meadows, O. M., Meadows, D. L. and Anders, J. appeared in 1972 and reinforced the fears of the environmentalists through the doomsday scenarios they presented.

Not surprisingly, this environmental movement found little support in the developing nations. Development and environmental conservation were portrayed as incompatible in that resources were thought to be finite; pollution and environmental deterioration were considered the inevitable consequences of industrial development. Many developing nations had only just gained independence and were sceptical regarding the motives behind proposals which seemed to limit their development objectives. These underdeveloped nations saw their development problems as being linked to too little industry rather than too much and contrasted this with the position of the developed countries which used the bulk of resources and contributed most to the resulting industrial pollution.

It was not until the mid-1970s that the fears of the developing countries were overcome and changing ideas of the environment ensured a greater participation of groups and nations from the developing world in the environmental debate. In 1971, the UN hosted a seminar on Environment and Development at Founex, Switzerland. There were two very important outcomes of this meeting. Firstly, there was a much more enlightened appreciation on the part of the international community of the position of the developing nations; their fears over the economic effects of environmental protection policies, their desire for industrialization as well as wider social and cultural development, and the nature of their own environmental problems. Secondly, the conception that environment and development problems were incompatible was overthrown as ideas of the environment were expanded from western concerns to include those which stem from a lack of development. By the 1972 UN Conference on the Human Environment, in Stockholm, the term 'pollution of poverty' was used to refer to the environmental concerns of the poor, such as lack of clean water or sanitation, which threatened life itself for many in the developing world.

Environment and development in the 1980s and 1990s

By the late 1970s, important changes in thinking regarding both the environment and development were causing the two previously separate issues to be seen as interdependent concerns. As a result, the interdependence of the developed and developing worlds was also recognized. The challenge for the 1980s was to formulate policies for action which would integrate the environment and development in practice. In 1980, the World Conservation Strategy (WCS) was published by the International Union for the Conservation of Nature and Natural Resources (IUCN), the United Nations Environment Programme (UNEP) and the World Wildlife Fund (now the World Wide Fund for Nature). For the first time, development was suggested as a major means of achieving conservation rather than an obstruction to it. Many countries in the developed and developing worlds have taken up the recommendations of the WCS to form National Conservation Strategies. However, despite its comprehensive and action-oriented nature, the WCS has been criticized for being 'repackaged 1970s environmentalism', through its commitment to neo-Malthusian population arguments and doomsday scenarios, and for underestimating the social and political challenges which would be necessary to implement the strategy. In contrast, the WCED report prioritizes the political and economic changes which will have to be made if sustainable development is to be achieved. The WCED report has, however, been referred to as 'comfortable reformism' and been criticized for not going far enough.

By 1992, the interdependent issues of environment and development were recognized to be of sufficient global concern to justify the largest assembly of heads of government in history at the UN Conference on Environment and Development in Rio de Janeiro, Brazil (the 'Earth Summit'). As one commentator noted, 'It is inspiring that they should have done so to discuss the environment, so that this word – one that has emerged only during the past few decades – has become a familiar concern in every country and almost every classroom in the world.'

Sustainable development is clearly a familiar term to many people in the developed nations and is on the political agendas of governments throughout the world. This book focuses on both the challenges of sustainable development and the opportunities for implementing sustainable development in the future. In Chapter 2, the impacts of past development processes on both people and the environments of the world are discussed. Overcoming poverty and 'cleaning up' the pollution caused by past productive activities are seen to be two of the primary challenges for all nations and not just individual countries.

In Chapter 3, the range of actions which have been taken at a variety of levels towards ensuring sustainable development in the future are identified. The ways in which people and places across the globe are interconnected are made explicit through consideration of the major issues of trade, aid and debt. The actions of national governments and Non-Governmental Organizations (NGOs) towards sustainable development are also highlighted. The fundamental future challenge of translating the substantial rhetoric which now surrounds sustainable development into practical actions is discussed.

In Chapters 4 and 5, the particular challenges and opportunities of sustainable development in the developing world are considered with respect to the rural and urban sectors. Addressing the welfare needs of the poorest groups is identified as being essential in order to achieve the goals of development and conservation in either sector. Some of the characteristics of projects which have met this challenge successfully are identified as the basis for future action in the developing world. The final chapter summarizes the progress made towards sustainable development and identifies the major ongoing challenges and opportunities for the future.

Conclusion

The origins of the concept of sustainable development have been seen to lie in two bodies of literature which in the 1960s were quite separate. As understanding of the challenges and achievements of both 'development' and the 'environment' changed, the two areas of study came closer together with the realization that environment and development were interdependent and mutually reinforcing issues.

In the course of such changes, representatives of governments from the developing world as well as the developed countries recognized their role and that of their populations in working towards sustainable development in the future. Not only are environment and development interdependent but also the achievement of sustainable development requires action on behalf of all peoples and places.

Key ideas

1 New patterns and processes of development are needed in the future if the development aspirations of the global community are to be met and the environment is to be conserved.

2 Sustainable development is a concept which encompasses the interdependent goals of development and environmental conservation.

3 In the 1960s, economic growth was thought to be the key to promoting development in the underdeveloped nations. This was an optimistic period in which the developing world, with the help of the developed countries, was to be integrated more fully into the world economy.

4 'Development' efforts in the 1970s became concerned with spreading the benefits of economic growth more widely amongst the population. It was also realized that a lack of development (i.e. poverty) was causing widespread environmental problems too.

5 There is a fundamental difference between the environmental concerns of the rich in the developed world, focusing on the 'quality of life', and those of the poor in the developing countries which focus on survival itself.

6 In the 1980s, development was for the first time put forward as a means of achieving conservation within the World Conservation Strategy.

2
The challenge of sustainable development

All forms of economic and social activity make demands on the resource base, whether agricultural production, industrial production or human settlements. If such activities are to be supported in the future, there is a need to ensure that resources such as fuels, water or soils are used with the greatest efficiency, that the by-products of these activities such as waste and pollution are kept to a minimum and that irreparable damage to the environment is not done. The call for sustainable development in the future has been seen to be a product of changes in thinking regarding both development and the environment such that these are now interdependent concerns. This chapter identifies some of the major characteristics of past processes and patterns of development and the impacts of these on the environment. This is essential to the understanding of the challenge of sustainable development, in terms of not only 'cleaning up' the effects of past development but also protecting the environment from further damage.

Inequalities in access to resources

The call for sustainable development in the future stems from a basic concern over the relationships between the current and projected population of the globe and the resource base which must support it. Malthus, writing at the end of the nineteenth century, was responsible for some very widely regarded (if gloomy) views on the future of a population growing 'geometrically' on a resource base which could only expand 'arithmetically'. These views continue to be both supported and countered. Generally, an intermediary position is now dominant in the debate over population numbers and the resource base for development.

It is not doubted that in some countries the ability of governments to provide basic needs for shelter, food, water and employment for their populations becomes increasingly difficult with rising numbers. For example, between 1975 and 1980, the population of India increased annually by over thirteen million (an average of 2 per cent per year), whereas that of the UK was only 21,000 per year (0.04 per cent). However, it is suggested that the overall population size may not be the most important factor in determining the prospects for sustainable development. The WCED states clearly the compromise view: 'Threats to the sustainable use of resources comes as much from inequalities in people's access to resources and from the ways in which they use them as from the sheer numbers of people.'

As will be seen in the following chapters, there is tremendous diversity in terms of people's access to resources. These can be considered at a variety of scales: differences within the household according to gender for example; inequalities within a local community; regional differences within a country such as between urban and rural populations and also at the international scale. Similarly, there are differences in the way people use resources which can also be considered at varying levels. For example, decisions regarding resource use differ between low and high income households, between public and private enterprise and within capitalist or socialist production. Case study B shows some of the characteristics of inequalities in the use of energy resources at these various scales.

Case study B

Inequalities in energy consumption

Energy can be derived from various sources (see Soussan in this series). A conventional distinction is made between commercial fuels, that is, modern fuels such as oil, coal, gas and electricity which have a commercial value and are often traded between countries, and non-commercial or traditional fuels such as wood, charcoal and plant/animal residues which are not usually bought or sold.

Case study B *(continued)*

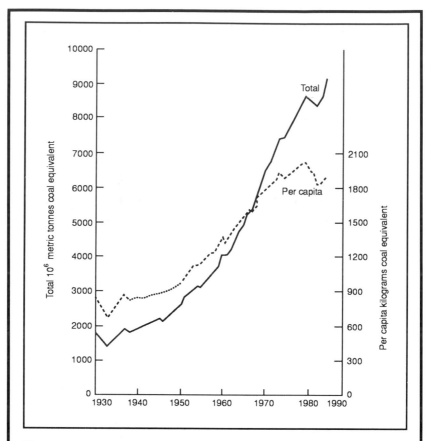

Figure 2.1 Global consumption of commercial energy
Source: Chapman, J. D. (1989) *Geography and Energy: Commercial Energy Systems and National Policies*, London: Longman.

Figure 2.1 portrays how global consumption of commercial energy has increased five-fold over the fifty years to 1987. The strong upward trend in energy consumed during the period resulted from the combination of population increase, economic expansion, rising incomes and a declining real cost of commercial energy sources (through economies of scale) up until the early

Case study B *(continued)*

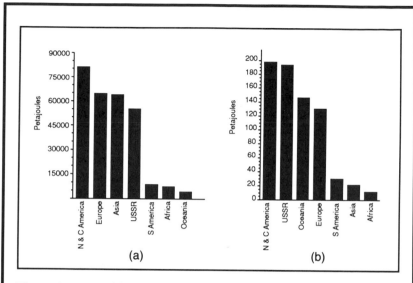

Figure 2.2 Total (a) and per capita (b) commercial energy consumption by major world region
Source: Chapman, J. D. (1989) *Geography and Energy: Commercial Energy Systems and National Policies*, London: Longman.

1970s. There was little concern for raising the efficiency of energy use at this time. Global consumption increased throughout the 1970s despite the increased real cost of fuels (particularly oil), only showing a decline in consumption in the early 1980s. Between 1980 and 1983, there was an annual decline in the consumption of commercial energy of 0.5–1.0 per cent owing to worldwide economic recession and very high energy prices.

Per capita consumption of commercial energy at the global scale exhibits a pattern very similar to that for total consumption. Not only has consumption increased over the period because of world population growth but also each individual on average now consumes more energy. Figure 2.2 shows the broad spatial patterns of consumption on a continental basis. North and Central America is seen to be the largest consumer of commercial energy in terms of both absolute consumption and per capita. Asia has a relatively

Case study B *(continued)*

large total consumption but energy consumed per capita is very small. In contrast, Oceania has a small total energy consumption but the average consumed per head of population is very large (greater than in Europe). However, in terms of change over time in the total and per capita consumption of commercial fuels, the rates are rising faster in the developing world than in other continents.

Despite the rising importance of commercial sources of energy in the developing world, for the majority of their citizens fuelwood or biomass sources remain the primary energy sources for heating and cooking. In Nepal, for example, 97 per cent of total energy consumption comes from fuelwood supplies (Soussan in this series). Similarly, Ethiopia and Burkina Faso rely on fuelwood for over 90 per cent of their total energy consumed. However, this international scale of analysis masks differences between and within countries.

In many areas of the developing world, both rural and urban, all energy sources have to be paid for. There are significant differences in total energy consumed and the relative importance of different sources according to level of income of the household. In general, low income groups spend a higher proportion of their income on fuel and the majority of this energy expenditure is on woodfuel. Higher income groups tend to have wider energy options, such as the use of kerosene, and spend a smaller proportion of their income on energy as a whole.

Research in rural India has also shown that the energy options are more restricted for lower income households. For example, those households which own land are able to obtain firewood (often paying hired labour to collect it) from their own trees, and are also able to use as energy sources residues from their crops and dung from the cattle they own. In contrast, the landless have to depend to a much greater extent on firewood and other biomass sources collected from forest or common land or from other people's land in return for work done. This is a common pattern; with growing poverty, the dependency on fuel collected from sources other than one's own increases.

Inequalities in access to resources threatens the prospects for sustainable development in many ways. Primarily, it confines large numbers of people to poverty which often leaves them with no choice but to degrade and destroy the resource base on which their future livelihoods depend. It is also such inequalities which allow a minority of people globally, within each nation and even at the community level, to use resources in a wasteful manner or in ways which causes environmental damage (such as polluting industries). The call for sustainable development in the future stems from the fact that such inequalities not only are morally wrong but also threaten the environmental basis for livelihoods and development aspirations across the globe.

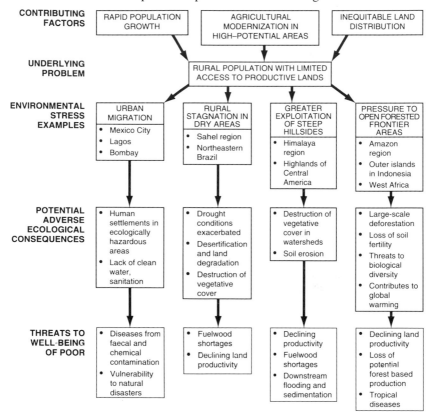

Figure 2.3 The poverty and environment connection
Source: Leonard, H. J. (1989) *Environment and the Poor: Development Strategies for a Common Agenda*, Oxford: Transaction Books.

The 'geographical retreat' of poverty

By the end of the 1970s, it was suggested that almost 40 per cent of the population of the developing countries lived in 'absolute poverty', defined in terms of income levels which were insufficient to provide adequate nutrition. The extent of poverty was found to be worst in those countries which had the lowest levels of GNP, yet high per capita incomes *per se* does not guarantee the absence of significant numbers of absolute poor. Todaro (1989) has observed that 'absolute poverty can and does exist as readily in New York City as it does in Calcutta, Cairo, Lagos or Bogotá, although its magnitude is likely to be much lower in terms of numbers or percentages of the total population.'

Figure 2.3 illustrates some of the linkages between poverty and the environment. It shows clearly how poverty can contribute to environmental stress, such as through the cultivation of steep hillsides. However, the relationship between poverty and the environment can be shown to be circular. The adverse ecological effects associated with people endeavouring to secure their basic needs in turn threaten the health and survival of those same people. The environmental concerns of the poor are those associated with immediate survival needs such as that for fuel or access to productive lands.

Plate 2.1 Poor people, poor environments
Source: Hamish Main, Staffordshire University

Furthermore, it is now realized that the world's poorest people are resident largely in the world's environmentally most fragile areas. This has been referred to as the 'retreat' of poverty into certain geographical areas; into remote and ecologically vulnerable rural areas or on the edges of growing towns. For example, when considering just the world's poorest groups (the poorest 20 per cent among the total population of all developing countries), 57 per cent of the rural poor and 76 per cent of the urban poor are resident in areas where ecological destruction and/or severe environmental hazards threaten their well-being. Case study C highlights starkly the interdependence of poverty and the environment for eighty families in urban Peru.

Sustainable development in the future will require a commitment to overcoming poverty through a focus on the welfare issues of the poorest sectors of society, particularly in the developing countries. Their environmental concerns and their development needs are associated with securing the most basic levels of economic and social well-being. Only through a global commitment to addressing these interdependent concerns of the poor will the environment be conserved or the development aspirations of individuals and nations be secured.

Case study C

Life amongst death on the top of the heap

The sky above the garbage dump is white with smoke and the sea across the polluted beach shines green with chemicals. Walter Tinco, aged four, is sorting shards of glass. His filthy hands toss the pieces on to piles that rise high above his head. His bare feet tread on a carpet of used toilet paper and torn nylon stockings.

About eighty families live in the dump at Callao, the sister port city to Lima, capital of Peru. They pay truck drivers to unload garbage near where they live and they use pigs, rakes and torches to search for bits of glass and metal, plastic bottles, old newspapers and bones, which they sell to buy food. Walter looked at a hut built of tin, rippled burlap and thatch. 'That's my home,' he said. After a day's work in the dump, nine-year-old Adela playfully chased the dogs that guard the beach from thieves. She said she likes living in the dump: 'You find all sorts of things: forks, comic books, dolls. It's fun. Once I found a silver ring.'

At least 2,000 people subsist by picking through Lima's garbage,

Case study C *(continued)*

according to a recent study. In a country where less than half of the people have enough to eat, they consider themselves lucky. 'The work is filthy, but we are honest, hard-working people,' said Victor Sanchez, who moved his family to the dump eight years ago. 'It's the only way we have to make a living.'

Drivers looking for a secluded place to empty their trucks started the unofficial Callao dump decades ago. It stretches for about a mile along the Oquendo beach behind the Bayer and El Pacifico chemical plants. A creek of acid, chlorine and mercury cuts through the dump to the beach, staining the sand and rocks before spilling into the Pacific Ocean. On the day Walter sorted the glass, two dog carcasses were rotting on its lime-green bank. 'Some days the chemical fumes make the people and pigs sick,' said Manuela Olivo, who lives nearby.

Mrs Olivo, standing in a small patch of bloody chicken feathers and human hair, tears apart small plastic bags of rubbish. Inside a driftwood fence, her dozen pigs fight over fruit rinds and fish heads. She said that the pigs would root in the new garbage for two or three days, then she and her family would spend a week or so raking and sorting the paper, plastic and cans.

Source: Guardian, 15.2.91.

The human cost of contemporary development

The need for sustainable development in the future is also confirmed by the human cost of contemporary patterns and processes of development. At present, fourteen million children under the age of five die annually in the developing world and this excludes deaths through famine. It is the poor who die young in all parts of the globe, and the poorest of all are children. Poor people in Europe or North America suffer more premature deaths than richer groups, but with a far higher proportion of people in poverty in the developing world the scale and severity of the problems of ill health and premature deaths are also greater. A child born in the developing world today is 15–20 times more likely to die before the age of five than a child born in western nations (see Table 2.1). Case study D elaborates on the spatial patterns of ill-health and premature death at a variety of scales.

Table 2.1 Percentage of children who do not survive to the age of five in selected countries

Country	Percentage
Afghanistan	32
Mali	29
Malawi	26
Chad	22
Nepal	20
Bangladesh	19
India	9
Brazil	8
Sri Lanka	4
Kuwait	2
USA	1.2
Norway	0.9

Source: World Resources 1990–91, World Resources Institute, Washington, DC.

Case study D

Spatial patterns of ill health

'Wealth determines health' is a phrase which is often used to explain the spatial pattern of ill health and premature death at various scales. Its popularity lies in its accuracy and application at several levels; internationally, to explain the differences already observed between countries of different levels of GNP in terms of child deaths before the age of five years, or nationally (as shown in Figure 2.4), where income levels, as expressed by social class, are seen to be closely related to premature deaths across all age groups in the United Kingdom.

Wealth determines health in terms not only of the ability of a nation to provide health services or the ability of individuals to pay for such services but also of determining the nature of the environment in which the majority of the population has to live. In the developing world in particular, additional characteristics of a healthy environment outside the provision of health care include supply of clean water, good sanitation facilities, safe housing or

Case study D *(continued)*

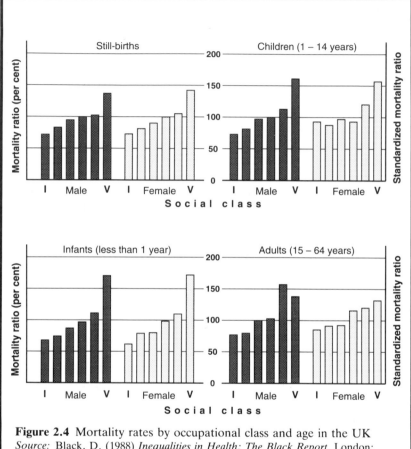

Figure 2.4 Mortality rates by occupational class and age in the UK
Source: Black, D. (1988) *Inequalities in Health: The Black Report*, London: Penguin.

freedom from hazardous installations, emissions or disease vectors. Yet poor people often live in the most unhealthy environments.

Of the fourteen million child deaths per year in the developing world, four million die of diarrhoeal diseases resulting from poor quality water and standards of sanitation. A further five million children die of diseases such as tetanus, whooping cough or

Case study D *(continued)*

measles, infections which in the presence of malnutrition become major killers in the developing world but which are now relatively minor causes of ill health in the developed nations. One million children die annually from malaria and others from a variety of illnesses often associated with the debilitating presence of malnutrition and worms.

In addition, children in the developing world are regularly cared for by parents who often have to grow food or make a living in environments within which the fundamental resource base is deteriorating. Exhausted soils produce smaller yields such that the quantity of food available to children may decline. Shortage of fuelwood for cooking is known to lead families to have less cooked meals or to switch to foodstuffs which require less cooking and are often less nutritious. Both trends will have detrimental effects on the nutritional status of children within these families.

Children also suffer most from the effects of pollution. A resting three-year-old consumes twice as much oxygen and therefore twice the pollution weight for weight as a resting adult. In addition, children's underdeveloped kidneys, livers and enzyme systems are less able to process such pollutants. Children's activities may also place them at particular risk; babies instinctively suck much of what they pick up in their hands and young children play in dangerous places such as streets or waste tips, aggravating the risk of contact with contaminated sources. Young children are responsible for very little pollution but are themselves extremely vulnerable to the pollution effects caused by others and, once again, it is impoverished children who are most at risk.

Inequalities in wealth go a long way towards explaining spatial patterns of ill health at several scales, but other factors are also important. For example, more children die before the age of five in Western Africa than in Eastern Africa. This has been linked to the prevalence of malaria in the former for which there is no reliable vaccine. In this instance, it is the particular environmental conditions of Western Africa, rather than regional differences in wealth, which explain such patterns.

Gender is another factor which cuts across inequalities in

Case study D *(continued)*

wealth. A distinctive feature of human health in developed countries is the longer life expectancy of women over men in all social classes. In the developing world, male children are often valued more highly than female. UNICEF declared 1990 as the Year of the Girl Child, reflecting the mounting concern for gender inequalities in countries such as India, where a recent survey has found that 300,000 more girls than boys die annually. Although female babies are generally born stronger than a male, within a month of birth the death rate of India's female babies is much higher than that of its males. It was found that girl children were receiving less priority in nutrition and health care and were breastfed less than boys. In 1988, a survey of 8,000 abortions, carried out in Bombay, found that 7,999 were female foetuses. These gender differences in premature deaths clearly cannot be explained by differences in wealth.

Current development patterns and processes are clearly not meeting the needs of children today and presents a gloomy prospect in terms of the likelihood of meeting the needs of future generations of children. Spatial inequalities in health have been seen to exist at all scales and show strong links with the distribution of wealth internationally between the developed and developing worlds, but also within nations. In the developing countries, trends throughout the 1980s show a decreased expenditure on health (by as much as 50 per cent per head in many of the poorest countries in Africa and Latin America) and on education (especially primary schooling). This is leading to an increasingly ill-educated as well as unhealthy young population. In addition, health has been seen to be closely tied to the physical environment, particularly in the developing world where poverty is so widespread and entrenched. Elimination of poverty and the provision of basic welfare needs for large numbers of people in the developing world must therefore form an essential basis for future development patterns and processes if this human cost of unsustainable development is to be avoided.

The environment cannot cope

Perhaps the starkest realization of the need to find new patterns and processes of development has come from improved understanding of the environmental unsustainability of contemporary development. All productive activities make demands on the resource base in terms of the raw materials on which they draw. In addition, all such activities involve some waste generation. These are termed the 'externalities' of production. Not all are harmful to the environment. Those which do endanger human health, harm ecosystems or interfere with other legitimate uses of the environment are termed 'pollutants'. In the last ten years, however, there has been increasing recognition of a series of environmental problems which extend across national boundaries and now affect the global community as a whole. Twenty years ago, the environmental sins of one country generally did not impinge on other nations. Since then, environmental problems, such as acid rain, have emerged which may affect a group of countries.

There is now a category of environmental problems which affects most if not all nations. Included in this category is the loss of biodiversity on the planet. As species become extinct, the cost is borne not only by the countries in which they once existed but also by humankind as a whole both today and in the future. One extinction may have many ramifications for other species in the complex food chains and webs which constitute the ecologies of the planet. In this way, the gene pool and therefore the potential opportunities for the discovery of new uses for such genes, within medicine for example, become restricted.

Also in this 'supranational' category of contemporary environmental issues is the problem of 'global warming', the heating up of the earth owing to the accumulation of 'greenhouse gases' (particularly carbon dioxide) in the earth's upper atmosphere. The predicted global rise in mean temperatures and sea levels and the varying impact on precipitation across the world ensure that all nations will be affected by global warming. The destruction of ozone in the stratosphere is also predicted to disrupt ecosystems across the globe and is therefore another supranational issue. Such issues, notes one commentator, 'deserve collective measures on the part of humankind as a whole'.

The legacy of past production

Productive activities in the modern world, whether agricultural or industrial, have been organized largely within two distinct models; that of capitalism and socialism. An understanding of the way in which productive activities are organized within societies is essential for understanding not only the impact of these activities on the environment but also the nature of the response taken in the past and the prospects for future conservation actions.

The capitalist mode of production

The capitalist mode of production has dominated the modern world. It began to replace feudalism in Western Europe from the sixteenth century onwards and expanded in the eighteenth century to include areas of the New World and other regions hitherto external to the capitalist centres of Western Europe. Capitalism depends on the continued raising of productivity and therefore such geographical expansion was necessary in order to secure new lands for agricultural production, new sources of industrial raw materials and new markets.

The impact on the environment of capitalist production is seen in many regions of the world. The defining characteristics of capitalism, such as the private ownership of resources, the need to maximize profits, and competition within a free-market economy, have in many cases led to the exploitation of environmental resources without sufficient concern for the long-term conservation of those resources or the environmental impact of such activities (which may not be seen in the short term). As more peoples and places became incorporated into the capitalist world economy (very directly in the case of settler colonialism), societies came under the same pressure to raise productivity and sell goods on the competitive market. The nature of these goods, however, was dictated by overseas rather than local needs and tastes. The cumulative effect was substantial change in the ecologies of these regions, the restructuring of social relationships between individuals and groups in society and greater demands on the physical environment. This process of incorporation did not end with colonialism and is very much part of the explanation of many of the contemporary environmental and development problems in the developing world.

The socialist mode of production

Socialism as a way of organizing production and society has its origins in what are termed 'primitive communist societies' in which resources were held communally and organized collectively on the basis of family or kinship obligations. Socialism developed as an ideology in the nineteenth century as a critique of capitalism built on the same basic

Figure 2.5 The environmental challenge in Eastern Europe: the case of Poland

In 1988 the Polish government declared five regions as disaster areas. The country is possibly the most polluted in Europe.

AIR   The economic crisis has meant increasing amounts of brown coal are burnt as alternative to other more expensive fuel sources. The worst affected areas are Upper Silesia and Kraków where sulphur dioxide deposits exceed 100 tonnes per square kilometre. A nuclear programme has been started and 15 per cent of energy needs are forecast to be met by nuclear power by 2000. In December 1989, the Solidarity government halted work on a major new nuclear plant near Gdańsk owing to concerns about the standards of technology and environmental impacts.

SOIL   Heavy metals have been found in vegetables grown in the most polluted areas. Unofficial estimates show that 60 per cent of food produced in the Kraków area is unfit for human consumption.

FORESTS   According to the UN Environment Programme 5–10 per cent of Polish forests are damaged but unofficial estimates suggest that the figure may be nearer 75 per cent. This is partly an imported problem: forests in the Tatry mountains in the south are being destroyed by acid pollution for Czechoslovakia and Silesia.

HEALTH   Incidents of cancer and bronchial illnesses are higher in polluted areas. Life expectancy is shorter and infant mortality higher than the national average.

INSTITUTIONS   There are institutes for environmental protection in Warsaw, Katowice, Wroclaw and Gdańsk. Pol-Eko was founded in 1988 by a British–Polish businessman, Stanley Adamski. There are numerous nature protection and ecological agencies. An international centre for the environment, supported by the EC, is planned for Gdańsk and the Baltic areas.

PROPOSALS   Assistance is being offered by the World Bank, USAID, Swedish International Development Agency, Holland, UK and West Germany. Some of this is already tied to specific projects. There is a high degree of theoretical knowledge and expertise but the major need is for advice on new technology, new legislation and funds for key projects.

Source: Guardian, 19.1.90.

principle of reciprocity as under primitive commmunism. However, obligations within socialism are to the state rather than family or kinship groups. Ownership of land and other productive resources, decisions regarding what is produced and how it is allocated, and to whom, are all made by the state (the representative body of the populace at large), on the basis of real needs and abilities. The socialist ideology denies that the market mechanism can lead to an equitable distribution of wealth across society.

Socialism has undergone substantial and rapid change in the last five years. In addition, the environmental legacy of socialist production is now becoming evident as political changes in Eastern Europe and the former USSR have 'opened up' these regions to external scrutiny and legitimized environmental groups in those countries. Figure 2.5 highlights just some of the challenges to sustainable development identified in one country, Poland.

Opportunities for pollution control

The ideological stance of the society in which productive activities take place has had an important influence on the nature of strategies adopted towards environmental conservation and pollution control. For example, under socialist forms of production, control over pollution strategies tends to be highly centralized and offers little opportunity for the monitoring or controlling of pollution by local authorities. This is in contrast to the situation under capitalist production in which such responsibility is often decentralized to regional and local authorities, as in the case of the UK with many aspects of pollution control.

The possibilities for public participation and scope for access to the political system by environmental groups also differ widely between the two ideologies. In the UK, for example, decision-making regarding pollution control is based on consultative procedures between ministers, various government advisory bodies and selected public advisory groups and individual consultants. Increasingly, representatives of environmental groups are being incorporated into the decision-making process too. This occurs through their co-option on to advisory boards and through public lobbying on environmental issues.

In contrast, in the USSR (prior to its breakup into independent states), most national policy-making of any importance took place in the Politburo and there was little recourse to the opinions of state agencies or local environmental needs. There was no political mechanism in the USSR to involve public groups or advisers within the decision-making process. The concentration of public environmental activities into a small number of government-sponsored groups also effectively minimized the prospects for any public pressure for environmental conservation. For the vast majority of the public, their awareness of environmental destruction, even in their local areas, was restricted by the secrecy of information in the USSR 'pre-glasnost'.

However, it is now recognized that no one system of production or administration of environmental control has the monopoly on conservation. Many commentators have suggested that environmental destruction was inevitable under capitalism, but that centrally planned economies would serve the interests of environmental protection better. However, as Goldman (1972) states, 'there is no reason to believe that state ownership of the means of production will necessarily guarantee the elimination of environmental disruption.'

Conclusion

Some degree of collective action has been fundamental to the survival of human societies throughout the history of civilization. For example, feudal societies were not self-sufficient or self-contained, but depended on much buying and selling within a system of local markets and trading centres. However, people and places today are connected in many more diverse and far-reaching ways (although at various intensities) within what can be termed the global economic system. Few places or people now remain unaffected to some degree by the actions of others, often at great distances away. Subsequent chapters highlight the ways in which features of the world economic system, such as international trade and aid flows, continue to shape resource use in diverse regions and societies. People are now dependent on cooperative interactions for survival which go far beyond those of original societies in terms of both number and complexity. In addition, the capacity to change the environment has risen dramatically with population increases and technological change, and has widened from their immediate surrounds as in early societies to the global environment itself in the modern world.

In summary, sustainable development is a challenge for people and planners across the globe rather than in isolation. It has been seen that the environmental challenge in terms of both rectifying the damage done through past development (e.g. global warming as a result of greenhouse gas emissions) and ensuring future conservation of resources (e.g. overcoming poverty) also ensures that the future fulfilment of development aspirations in any one region is dependent on collective actions of all societies across the globe. In continuity with the operation of all systems, a change in any one element within the global economic system has implications for the functioning of the system as a whole. The challenge of sustainable development is to ensure that the relationships (all of the economic, political, and social connections) between elements in the system (the people and places) are such that economic growth is achieved whilst the environment is also conserved.

Key ideas

1 It is the inequalities in people's access to resources and the way in which they use them that are a greater threat to sustainable development in the future than population growth itself.
2 Current patterns and processes of development are unsustainable in that they confine large numbers of people, mainly in the developing world, to ill health and premature death.
3 There is a category of environmental problems termed 'supranational' in that they extend across national boundaries and affect the global community as a whole.
4 Primitive communist societies had a minimal impact on the environment. This is not the case in socialist societies in which extensive environmental degradation is evidenced.
5 The continual need to raise production within capitalism has led to environmental impacts throughout the world.
6 No one system of production or administration of pollution control has the monopoly on conservation. Sustainable development in the future is a global challenge.

3
Action towards sustainable development

Accepting the necessity and desirability of sustainable development in the future was the essential prerequisite for the global community to start taking action. Measures taken by actors at various spatial scales with the explicit aim of moving towards sustainable development have escalated over the last five years. In so doing, however, the real challenges of sustainable development, that of reconciling the ambitions of various interest groups, of identifying basic versus extravagant needs and of balancing present and future development aspirations, have all become clearer. Inevitably, the practice of sustainable development is proving more difficult than professing an ideological commitment, yet there are signs of progress.

This chapter identifies some of the progress which has been made. The focus is on actions taken at various levels, from national governments to Non-Governmental Organizations. In subsequent chapters, the analysis is of actions taken within particular sectors, urban and rural.

Questions of responsibility and response

Who is the polluter, who should pay?

The interdependence today of peoples and environments throughout the world is seen most clearly in the specific environmental problems,

Plate 3.1 The transfer of pollution downwind
Source: Gordon Walker, Staffordshire University

that are termed supranational. The need for a coordinated international response with respect to such environmental issues is self-evident. But, in the moves to determine the response to such problems, the question of responsibility is inevitably raised. If change is to be implemented, particularly where such change involves (as it usually does) expense and/or compromise of some sort, there is substantial debate as to whether these costs should be borne equally by all or whether there should be some adjustment according to relative responsibility (if this can be ascertained) and also ability to pay.

Pollution effects are often spatially and temporally removed from the site of production; they may only be felt far downstream or downwind and perhaps only in the next agricultural season or even several years later. Case study E illustrates how the costs of production are not necessarily borne by those who received the benefits. It is this characteristic of the externalities of production often being spatially and temporally removed from the production site which constitutes one of the fundamental challenges for ensuring sustainable productive activities in the future.

Case study E

The export of hazardous wastes

Between 1986 and 1991, 175 million tonnes of hazardous waste was offered on the world market. Hazardous waste is defined as waste which, if deposited into landfills, air or water in untreated form, will be detrimental to human health or the environment. It includes toxic materials, flammables, explosives, carcinogenics and nuclear materials. Ten million tonnes of such wastes were exported between 1986 and 1991, largely from the industrialized countries to the developing world. The main receiving areas today

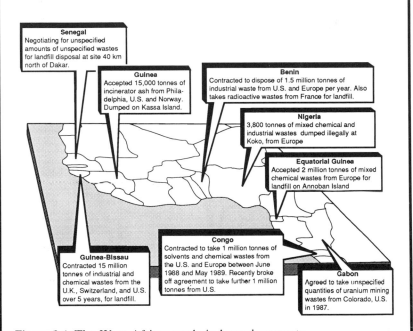

Senegal
Negotiating for unspecified amounts of unspecified wastes for landfill disposal at site 40 km north of Dakar.

Guinea
Accepted 15,000 tonnes of incinerator ash from Philadelphia, U.S. and Norway. Dumped on Kassa Island.

Benin
Contracted to dispose of 1.5 million tonnes of industrial waste from U.S. and Europe per year. Also takes radioactive wastes from France for landfill.

Nigeria
3,800 tonnes of mixed chemical and industrial wastes dumped illegally at Koko, from Europe

Equatorial Guinea
Accepted 2 million tonnes of mixed chemical wastes from Europe for landfill on Annoban Island

Guinea-Bissau
Contracted 15 million tonnes of industrial and chemical wastes from the U.K., Switzerland, and U.S. over 5 years, for landfill.

Congo
Contracted to take 1 million tonnes of solvents and chemical wastes from the U.S. and Europe between June 1988 and May 1989. Recently broke off agreement to take further 1 million tonnes from U.S.

Gabon
Agreed to take unspecified quantities of uranium mining wastes from Colorado, U.S. in 1987.

Figure 3.1 The West African trade in hazardous waste
Source: Third World Network (1989) *Toxic Terror: Dumping of Hazardous Wastes in the Third World*, Penang: Third World Network.

Case study E *(continued)*

are the Caribbean and Central and South America, with huge growth in shipments to the former Soviet states. Figure 3.1 illustrates aspects of the recent trade in hazardous wastes in West Africa.

This explosion over recent years in the export of hazardous waste is a product of two main factors; the uneven progress in the development of environmental standards throughout the world and the rise of the free market economy. In the West, consumer demand for clean industry has led to more and more stringent rules concerning the treatment, storage and disposal of toxic waste materials. The added cost associated with adherence to these regulations as well as the lack of land in countries such as Britain to receive the growing volume of wastes, has led to companies taking the easy option; the dumping of toxic wastes in poor countries with large areas of land and with few restricting regulations on disposal. Such practices are supported by institutions such as the World Bank and the General Agreement on Tariffs and Trade. Recent communications from these institutions suggests that the waste trade is seen as an important wealth earner for the developing countries and that hazardous wastes, like any other commodity, should be allowed to move across borders within a free market economy.

Currently, the export of toxic wastes to the developing world takes place as a result of both legal contracts and illegal dumping. The short-term monetary gains from importing toxic wastes are attractive to individual companies and governments of poor countries alike. For example, two British firms offered US$120 million per year to Guinea-Bissau to bury industrial waste material. This is equivalent to the annual GNP of that country. In the Congo, a number of individuals agreed to import one million tonnes of industrial waste from Holland which would have made US$4 million over three years. These amounts paid to the receiver are negligible, however, compared to the savings made on storage and disposal in the country of origin. The sum of US$40 per tonne was paid to Guinea importers of toxic industrial ash from Philadelphia. Storage in the USA in compliance with government regulations would have cost the company US$1,000 per tonne.

Case study E *(continued)*

Awareness is growing of the intractable nature of the toxic waste problem; the difficulty of making toxic wastes safe and the time span over which many materials, particularly nuclear wastes, remain dangerous are now more fully appreciated. The disposal of such products presents a substantial technological as well as political challenge. The economic, health and environmental costs of past mistakes are only just being realized. In the USA in 1980, the President's Council on Environmental Quality estimated that the cost of cleaning up existing dump sites in the country would be US$28–55 billion. In the UK, the cost of dismantling and disposing of redundant nuclear installations is estimated to be £20 billion. In the case of the latter, a site for the necessary deep repository is still to be found; the political considerations of where this should be are inevitably as difficult as the scientific and geological factors.

The developing nations are even more ill-equipped than the industrialized countries to deal with toxic wastes. Very rarely is the awareness or technology available in these countries for handling the long or short-term dangers of these materials. In 1988, the Organization of African Unity passed a resolution calling for a ban on the importation of hazardous wastes to the continent. Individual countries have reversed earlier agreements to import wastes, and movements to Africa are now confined to South Africa and Morocco. The United Nations Environment Programme has drawn up a list of forty-four core materials considered to be hazardous and recommends that the importing country should show evidence of its capacity to deal with the particular waste prior to any trade.

However, the effects of such a treaty will remain minimal until there is a body which can assess and monitor the capability of countries to handle these materials. Similar directives on dumping have been issued by the EC but, at present, there are no international norms on what is proper waste treatment. There are no moves by any industrialized country or international institution to ban waste exports and, in consequence, the trade in hazardous materials continues to expand.

One way in which it is thought that pollution may be minimized is to make those who cause pollution bear the costs of rectifying the damage done. This is what is termed the 'Polluter Pays Principle'. However, the operation or implementation of such a principle has several problems. First, it requires the identification of who is responsible, and to what extent, for the production of these harmful substances or effects. In addition, it depends on being able to 'cost' the damage done. Conventional 'cost–benefit analyses', which are used in a variety of areas of planning, have been based on assigning a market value to resources and their degradation.

One example will serve to illustrate the problems of implementing the polluter pays principle in practice. 'Acid rain' is a term used to refer to the abnormally low pH of some rainfall resultant from the concentration of primarily sulphur dioxide. Scientists in Scandinavia have linked damage to trees, buildings and aquatic ecosystems in their countries to the burning of fossil fuels (leading to acid rain) within industry located in the UK and elsewhere in Europe. But it is not possible to apportion the blame for such pollution to particular countries, industries or individual companies. In addition, whilst it may be possible to cost the damage to trees in terms of the loss of timber resources, it is much more difficult to assign a market value to the loss of diversity of flora and fauna supported by such forests or to their decreased amenity value with regard to recreational opportunities lost for the local population as a result of acid rain.

The fact that pollution effects are often not felt immediately provides additional problems for the implementation of the polluter pays principle and for sustainable development in the future. Once again, it is uncertainty and a lack of understanding of pollution effects which constrains actions for prevention and control. Some substances become hazardous to peoples and environments only after a certain time or when they have built up to a threshold level, for example nitrates in soil and water. Moreover, there is often substantial disagreement within the scientific community over what these thresholds are and the nature of the link between the particular externality of production and the ill health of ecosystems and humans. Nuclear waste is one case in which the pollution effect is considered to decrease over time but, again, there is controversy regarding the length of time taken for such products to become harmless.

It is this problem of a lack of understanding regarding the links between cause and effect in the production and impact of pollution which represents a major challenge for ensuring that future productive activities at all levels are sustainable.

The power to respond

In Chapter 2, it was noted that the environmental concerns of the poor are related to survival itself. This applies as much to poor countries as it does to their low-income populations. Clearly, it is unrealistic to expect poor people to conserve resources for the future when they are struggling for survival. The governments of these countries, in turn, have very scarce economic resources for any activities outside the provision of basic human needs. It is not only on moral grounds, therefore, that rich countries should demonstrate their political will to tackle poverty in the developing countries, but also on a practical basis.

The question of the relative power of individual nations to participate in actions towards sustainable development is also raised with respect to the future development patterns and processes in the newly independent countries of Eastern Europe. These countries face severe economic challenges in the future, together with substantial environmental problems (see Figure 2.5). The developed world is likely to play an important role in the prospects for future sustainable development in this region. A recent article in the *Guardian* concluded that 'Drastic measures are required. Eastern Europe cannot afford to fund them and the West cannot afford to stand by and watch. This is not just a moral obligation. It is in the West's interest.' However, the nature of any prospective intervention is also critical. For example, a member of the Hungarian Green Party is concerned that 'third-rate Soviet technology, which poisoned us for forty years, will now be replaced by second-rate technology from the West – sold cheaply to us because it is too polluting for them.'

Implications for sovereignty

At the time of the UN Conference on the Human Environment in 1972, it was individual nations in the main who decided how the resources within their boundaries would be used. By and large, environmental problems were limited to individual nations or a small group of nations. However, the more recent acceptance of the principle that all nations have responsibility for the health of the planet raises questions of sovereignty and the right to decide how a nation's resources will be used.

In Chapter 1 it was noted that the initial hesitancy of developing nations to participate in the environmental debates of the 1960s was due in part to concern over the loss of control over their own development. These same fears are resurfacing within international negotiations to determine actions for sustainable development. For example, the Brazilian government has repeatedly voiced its view that the future of the Amazon rainforest is strictly its own affair. The aspirations of Chinese and Indian citizens for refrigeration, and their consequent reluctance to commit themselves to international codes for CFC reductions, are similarly well reported.

The reconciliation of these questions of responsibility and response is critical to sustainable development in the future. They are issues which resurface many times in the subsequent sections of this chapter as challenges to the implementation of sustainable development. If, in the name of environmental conservation, the populations of the developing countries are to be denied the same route to material well-being that the developed world enjoyed, the responsibility for finding and funding alternatives which are sustainable cannot be left to these individual nations alone. Only through fair and open negotiations over such actions will the fears of the developing nations be proven unfounded and real prospects for sustainable development be ensured. Case study F illustrates these questions which have underpinned international action towards combating global warming.

Case study F

Responsibility and response in combating global warming

In April 1990, the *Independent* predicted that 'Greenhouse diplomacy' would come to dominate international relations by the late 1990s. The process has already started with a series of conferences, declarations, intergovernmental panels and treaties, all focused on trying to disentangle the question of who puts what in the atmosphere and what they should do about it.

Underpinning all of these international conferences is the concern for, firstly, the impact of current emissions of 'greenhouse gases' (those gases such as carbon dioxide which are known to cause global warming) on the environment and, secondly, the prospective impact of future emissions, particularly if the developing

---

Case study F *(continued)*

world follows the same patterns and processes of industrial development. For example, the burning of fossil fuels is a primary contributor to the increasing content of carbon dioxide in the atmosphere. China is 76 per cent dependent on coal for its energy and currently uses over one billion tonnes per annum. China envisages expanding its coal consumption to three billion tonnes per year by 2020 and this alone would add nearly 50 per cent to current world carbon emissions. A World Wide Fund for Nature representative stated recently that it is not just the health of China's people which is at stake: 'What the rest of the world does about energy and the environment will be irrelevant if China gets it wrong.'

It is estimated that a 50–80 per cent reduction in emissions of carbon dioxide is required to stabilize atmospheric concentrations at the current levels. In terms of other greenhouse gases, reductions above 80 per cent are needed for CFCs and nitrous oxide, although it is estimated that a 10–20 per cent reduction in methane will stabilize atmospheric concentrations. Although the level of action required is relatively clear, the debate continues as to who is responsible in terms of both emissions and the necessary response. Focusing on carbon dioxide as the major greenhouse gas and one which can be very directly related to levels of fossil fuel use and deforestation, Table 3.1 shows the responsibility for global warming on behalf of the major regions of the world (when all greenhouse gases are accounted for) and amongst individual countries (based on carbon emissions). The major responsibility is seen to lie with a minority of the world's population, in the west. More specifically, the average American citizen is responsible for nine times the emission of carbon dioxide as the average Chinese citizen.

The battle of statistics is an extremely important one, since potential solutions to the problem will be argued on the different figures. Questions of who *should* pay are being argued on the basis of the evident divergence between the developed and developing world in terms of responsibility for current emissions. When figures are expressed as in Table 3.1 in relation to GNP, the

Case study F *(continued)*

Table 3.1 Carbon culprits

Total emissions of greenhouse gases

Regions	World population (%)	Responsibility for global warming (%)
The West	15	46
USSR/Eastern Europe	7	19
Third World	78	35

Fossil fuel carbon emissions (1987)

Country	Amount (million tons)	Per $ GNP (grams)	Per person (tons)
USA	1224	276	5.03
Canada	110	247	4.24
Australia	65	320	4.00
USSR	1035	436	3.68
Saudi Arabia	45	565	3.60
Poland	128	492	3.38
W. Germany	182	223	2.98
UK	156	224	2.73
Japan	251	156	2.12
France	95	133	1.70
S. Korea	44	374	1.14
Mexico	80	609	0.96
China	594	2024	0.56
Egypt	21	801	0.41
Brazil	53	170	0.38
India	151	655	0.19
Indonesia	28	403	0.16
Nigeria	9	359	0.09

Source: New Internationalist, April 1990.

question of who is *able* to pay also becomes paramount. What is certain is that, whatever measure is chosen, countries vary greatly in terms of both past and current contributions. In addition, the implications and costs of limiting emissions and the possible impact of global warming may vary greatly between countries.

Given these factors, an 'equal reductions' agreement world-wide, as a means of reducing greenhouse gas emissions, would be very hard to negotiate. Some nations would argue (as Japan has done) that they have already taken steps to limit emissions and

Case study F *(continued)*

therefore should not be expected to reduce further to the same extent as other countries. Other nations, such as the USA, could reduce emissions relatively easily through improvements in efficiency or by switching towards alternative energy sources other than coal. All countries are likely to find reasons to argue that their reductions should be less than average. The USA, for example, is already arguing that its large continental land mass is such that energy demands through transport are higher. In addition, the USA points to the energy requirements associated with its operation of a large part of the West's military forces.

Alternative options for reconciling both the responsibility and the ability of nations to take action to reduce global warming are being considered. Carbon taxes are one such option. The basic idea is simple; applying a tax to emissions of carbon would encourage processes which lead to low or zero carbon production and discourage those with higher carbon production. Such taxes could be used at the international level to create a fund which could then be used to finance research and development into ways of further reducing carbon emissions. This has been suggested by the European Community. At a national level, a carbon tax could be part of a move away from taxes on income (as is usually the case at present) to taxes on consumption, pollution and resources. The EC is currently drawing up proposals to encourage individual nations to levy such a tax (the EC has no tax raising powers itself). There is substantial resistance on the part of individual member countries, however, as they fear that a unilateral application of a carbon tax would make their industries less competitive.

A second means to limit carbon emissions is to restrict the amount of fossil fuels which may be produced. This could be effected through setting production quotas. Prices of fossil fuel energy would rise but, in so doing, would offset some of the losses to individual producers of reduced production. A major problem, however, would be that production would be sought from the cheapest sources and go to the highest bidder. In this way, the most damaging activities could become the most profitable. In addition, such production quotas would concentrate wealth with

Case study F *(continued)*

the energy producers and create enormous international political and economic problems associated with this process and the rise in energy prices.

The third option is to control carbon emissions through a system of 'permits to emit'. The total number of permits issued worldwide would correspond to what the environment could tolerate, but individual permits could be traded between countries on the free market. There are many questions to be resolved before such a system could become operational, such as how permits would be allocated and whether they should be leased or traded permanently. The developing nations advocate a scenario in which each country would prepare a budget of greenhouse emissions to set against the size of its population and the ability of its environment to absorb such emissions (related to characteristics of the soil and vegetation). Compensation would then be paid by those who are over the permitted level to those who are under it. It is estimated that if over-producers paid $15 per 1,000 tonnes of excess, 20 developing countries would receive approximately $30 billion. It has been recommended that such payments would not be in cash, but in the form of development aid and conservation technologies from the industrialized countries to the developing world.

It is thought that such tradable emission permits represent the most hopeful and fair means of stabilizing global greenhouse emissions. It so doing, poor nations would be allowed to increase their consumption of fossil fuels, but would receive help in using them as efficiently as possible.

International action

Perhaps our most urgent task today is to persuade nations of the need to return to multilateralism . . . after a decade and a half of a standstill or even deterioration in global cooperation, the time has come for higher expectations, for common goals pursued together, for an increased political will to address our common future.

(WCED 1987)

Since the report of the World Commission on Environment and Development was published, a number of actions have been taken by the international community in an attempt to foster collaboration in addressing the environmental and development challenges which stretch across national boundaries. National governments from both the developed and developing worlds, for example, have come together since 1987 to commit themselves to various protocols, treaties and conventions on issues which face the global community as a whole.

In 1987, UNEP, for example, brought government representatives together in Montreal to consider a protocol on substances that deplete the ozone layer. Governments representing two-thirds of global CFC use agreed to targets for the phasing out of such substances, and the 'Montreal Protocol' became effective in 1989. In 1987, UNEP also established an Intergovernmental Panel on Climate Change (IPCC) to coordinate research and to identify response strategies to global warming.

In addition, environmental issues such as deforestation, species loss and the management of Antarctica have received international attention. The International Tropical Timber Organization (ITTO) has 45 member countries who account for 80 per cent of these forests and 95 per cent of tropical timber exports. All members are signatories to an agreement on the production and use of tropical timber and are committed to finding better and sustainable forest management techniques. The Convention on International Trade in Endangered Species of Wild Flora and Fauna (CITES) was established in 1973 and continues to be the major international monitoring force on species loss. In 1992, it added the African elephant to its list of endangered species and introduced a controversial ban on the sale of ivory in an attempt to limit poaching of these animals. There have also been efforts at the international level to enact a Convention on the Regulation of Antarctic Minerals Resources Activity but, to date, the details of this have not been resolved amongst signatories.

Regional groupings, such as the Non-Aligned Movement (NAM), members of the Commonwealth and the Group of Seven, have also taken on the challenge of sustainable development and the need for coordinated activities amongst their members. In 1989, the heads of state or governments of the non-aligned countries declared their commitment to accelerated economic and social development of the developing countries, which is a prerequisite for sustainable development. Many of these same leaders, those of the Commonwealth, later in the same year committed themselves to a sixteen-point programme of action on specific matters such as energy conservation, sustainable forest management and the need to develop international funding mechanisms for environmental cooperation.

Similarly, in 1989, leaders from the industrialized nations of Canada, France, Italy, Japan, the United Kingdom, the United States and West Germany (the Group of Seven) met at their annual economic summit and acknowledged that environmental threats must be given equal priority to economic ones in their future activities. One-third of the 56 paragraphs in their final communiqué had the word 'environment' within their headings (as compared to three in the previous year).

However, concern should be measured by actions rather than declarations. The following sections highlight some of the major steps taken within the international community to foster sustainable development.

Aid and the environment

Foreign aid is defined as any flow of capital to the developing nations which meets two criteria. First, its objective should be non-commercial from the point of view of the donor; second, it should be characterized by interest and repayment terms which are less stringent than those of the commercial world. The concept of foreign aid is that these grants and loans are broadly aimed at transferring resources from wealthy to poor nations on the grounds of development or income redistribution.

There is substantial debate over the impact of Overseas Development Assistance (ODA) on the recipient nations. Opinions range from the belief that it is an essential prerequisite for development, supplementing scarce domestic resources, to the view that aid perpetuates neo-colonial dependency relationships which will ensure that recipient nations remain underdeveloped. In terms of the impact of aid on the environment, in recent years a number of aid projects have been shown to have highly negative effects. In particular, resettlement projects, large dams and road building have caused widespread damage to environments and local peoples. The growing recognition, however, that partnership between industrial and developing countries is indispensable to achieving sound environmental management on a global scale is prompting changes amongst both donors and recipients of aid. Donor governments are now responding to pressures from their own peoples as much as from the international community to ensure that future funds are used for environmentally sustainable projects. The governments of recipient nations are also turning to sources of foreign funds and advice as they become aware of the costs and complexities of environmental protection.

The World Bank (the International Bank for Reconstruction and Development) is the major source of multilateral funds for the developing countries. In addition, for each dollar that the World Bank lends, it can be expected that another two to three dollars will also flow to these projects from other agencies, from private banks and from the recipient governments. The rhetoric and actions of the World Bank towards the environment are therefore crucial in determining the prospects for sustainable development.

In its progress report for 1991 on the 'World Bank and the Environment', it is stated that the speedy integration over the previous five years of environmental concerns into the Bank activities is in recognition that 'mounting environmental degradation threatens the attainment of the Bank's main objectives: reducing poverty and promoting sustainable development'. Some commentators would dispute not only whether these objectives were truly the World Bank's key intentions but also the degree to which the World Bank's actions reflect such objectives. In May 1991, for example, the USA threatened to withhold 25 per cent of its 1992 contribution to the World Bank (approximately $70 million) until it was satisfied that the Bank was serious about implementing environmental reforms into its lending activities.

The World Bank lends money to individual governments for specific projects. These projects are identified and designed by the government of the recipient nation. These governments are expected to contribute a portion of the funds for the proposed project and the project itself is expected to earn a profit. It has been some of the World Bank's largest projects which have attracted the most attention from environmentalists. For example, case study G highlights the continuing uncertainty surrounding the bank's involvement in the damming of the Narmada in India.

Case study G

Damming the Narmada in India

In 1987, work started on the Sadar Sarovar dam, one of the two principal dams of the US$5 billion Narmada Valley Project in India. The location of the project is shown in Figure 3.2. The assent for the project came from the government of Prime

Case study G *(continued)*

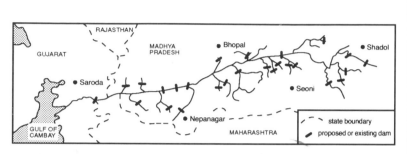

Figure 3.2 Major existing and proposed dam sites in the Narmada Basin
Source: Alvares, C. and Billoney, R. (1988) *Damming the Narmada: India's Greatest Planned Environmental Disaster*, Penang: Third World Network.

Minister Rajiv Gandhi after twenty years of political wrangling over the apportionment of costs and benefits of the scheme.

The scheme is the world's largest hydroelectric and irrigation complex, based on 30 major, 135 medium and 3,000 minor dams to be built over fifty years. As well as generating an estimated 500 million megawatts of electricity, it is designed to irrigate over two million hectares and bring drinking water to thousands of villages. The scheme, however, remains shrouded in controversy.

The Narmada is India's fifth largest river, rising in Madhya Pradesh and flowing westward to the Arabian sea over 1300 km away. It is currently home to twenty million people and the destination for hundreds of thousands of Hindu pilgrims each year who visit the shrines along its banks. All Hindu inhabitants of the valley are supposed to walk the entire length of the river at least once in their lifetime.

The Narmada Valley scheme has been referred to as an environmental catastrophe, a technological dinosaur and an example of flagrant social injustice. The dams will displace 200,000 people, submerge 2,000 sq. km of fertile land and 1,500 sq. km of prime teak and sal forest, and eliminate historic sites and rare wildlife. The expansion of irrigated agriculture is likely to leave impoverished farmers upstream with even less water than before.

The World Bank, which is the largest source of funds for the

Case study G *(continued)*

scheme, has had four reviews in the two-year period of construction of the Sadar Sarovar dam. Its concern is for the lack of effective planning, on behalf of the Indian government, for resettlement of inhabitants of the surrounding area. The $70 million loan towards resettlement and the $350 million for the dam itself are on hold 'awaiting resolution of outstanding issues'. One suggestion from Survival International is that the Indian government has still not identified land for resettlement because there is no land. Almost all cultivatable land in the region is already farmed and the remainder is too poor for permanent cultivation.

In addition, the Narmada is in a seismic zone in which thirty earthquakes have shaken the region in the last 200 years. The sheer weight of the new giant reservoirs could trigger an earthquake in a zone of known fractures and faults such as the Narmada basin.

Resistance to the project from diverse groups under threat by this and other schemes has been shown in a number of strikes and demonstrations. The anti-dam movement has been referred to as India's first nationwide environmental protest. Hundreds of people were arrested in December 1990 after a 200 km protest march from the main dam site to the villages where most of those to be relocated live.

The debate and the disputes are likely to continue. As public protest mounts both within India and overseas, the political interests of various groups will become clear. The World Bank has to juxtapose its role as a money-making institution with international demands for a greener and more socially aware lending body. The government of India will have to balance its need and desire to maintain the favours of the landed élite (who are deemed likely to be the major beneficiaries of the irrigation programmes) with the popular opposition which has become a national alliance.

It has been suggested that a lowering of the Narmada Sagar dam wall from 139 m to 128 m would reduce population displacement by 90 per cent and reprieve 80 per cent of the cultivated land from submersion. But, since the original size of the project reflected the need to accommodate the aspirations of four rival states, it is unlikely that any will be willing to see a reduction in their benefits now.

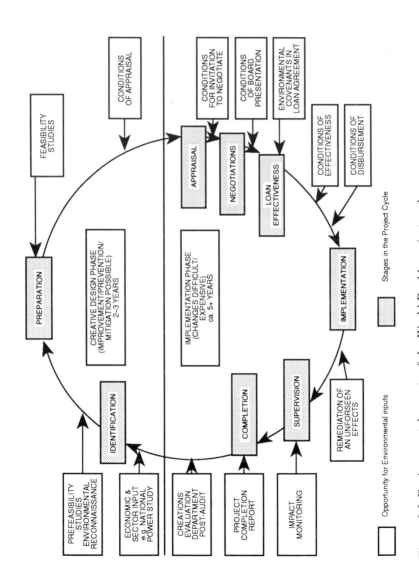

Figure 3.3 Environmental aspects of the World Bank's project cycle
Source: Goodland, R. J. A. (1990) 'Environment and development: progress of the World Bank', *Geographical Journal* 156 (2).

The World Bank is slowly moving away from its emphasis on major projects. The mounting evidence that environmental stress can actually reduce the economic advantages of some projects, by shortening their life expectancy and by stimulating side-effects such as soil erosion, has undoubtedly been important in prompting this change. In addition, there are attempts to ensure that each project is environmentally sustainable in future by a number of inputs at various stages in the 'project cycle', as shown in Figure 3.3.

In addition to this 'project-by-project' approach, the World Bank is assisting governments in building environmental concerns into policy making at all levels. Since 1988, all Country Strategy Papers which the Bank prepares with host countries have contained sections on the key constraints to sustainable development within the region. All countries to which the Bank lends also have an Environmental Issues Brief detailing the environmental and natural resource conditions for the country. Such initiatives are helping to ensure that the environment is integrated into all sectors of a country's macroeconomic policy and in its dialogue with the World Bank. In addition, the Bank assists countries in the production of National Environmental Action Plans through the Regional Divisions of its Environment Department. The full range of both international and local, private and public institutions participate in the formulation of these plans, which deal with national ecological, social and economic conditions.

The World Bank is also now encouraging alliance with NGOs who traditionally have been vociferous opponents of the World Bank. This is in recognition of the evident success of in-country NGOs in areas such as the involvement of local citizens and in the monitoring of environmental quality.

Such developments do represent progress towards institutional reform and a greater emphasis within donor lending on poverty reduction, popular participation and sustainable development. However, as the Director of Oxfam stated recently, 'Even the most appropriate aid is undermined if it's not combined with better terms of trade for the developing world and significant debt reduction.'

Trade and the environment

Recognition of the environmental impact of trade policies was one of the hallmarks of the WCED report. Nevertheless, recent developments in the regulation of international trade, particularly the evidence emerging from the latest round of GATT negotiations (the General

Agreement on Tariffs and Trade), have not given much hope for a substantial reordering of the existing relationships between the developed and developing nations in this arena.

Approximately 90 per cent of international trade is regulated under GATT, which embodies a number of agreements negotiated between its membership of 103 countries. GATT was established in 1947, with a view to engineering the post-war economic reconstruction, in conjunction with the UN and the World Bank, through the vigorous promotion of free trade. GATT has phases of greater action, known as 'Rounds', in which countries negotiate to liberalize world trade through reducing import and export controls and by eliminating trade barriers. There have been seven complete Rounds since GATT's inauguration and the latest, known as the Uruguay Round, started in September 1986 and was due to conclude in December 1990.

GATT (in common with the World Bank) believes that all trade is good trade. Any obstacle to its expansion therefore is considered harmful. Essentially, the environment is viewed as a mass of raw materials to be processed and marketed, preferably through the international trading system, to increase GNP. Low environmental standards (natural resources, low wages and plentiful land) are viewed as one element in a country's comparative advantage to be exploited through trade. The principle of comparative advantage suggests that if each country were to concentrate on what it produced best, everyone would gain from the growing volume of world trade. According to this view, however, the sharing of wealth depends on a genuinely free international market. GATT aims to ensure this through the promotion of two key principles. The first is of 'national treatment' under which countries must treat participants in their economies the same as domestic firms. The second principle is the 'most favoured nation' which states that any concession granted by a GATT member to any one trading partner must be extended to all.

Emerging evidence from the Uruguay Round suggests an apparent neglect of consideration for the environmental impact of GATT policies. In rhetorical terms, the word 'environment' is virtually absent from GATT statements. Despite the formation of a Trade and Environment Committee in 1971, this committee has never met. In addition, there are a number of proposals which appear likely to compromise moves towards sustainable development through their indirect and direct impact on the environment. These policies have been referred to in the *Guardian* as a 'trade pact likely to usher in a new phase of ecological destruction and deepening food insecurity'.

For example, to date, individual countries have been able to limit exports in order to protect a particular natural resource. Indonesia banned the export of raw logs in 1985, which has served to encourage value-added manufacturing within the country and reduce pressure on its rainforests. It is likely, however, that such controls will become outlawed as a result of the Uruguay Round and will leave Indonesia with a choice between ecologically damaging free trade in raw timber or comprehensive trade sanctions by GATT members.

The ban on export controls is also likely to be extended to agricultural commodities. The implications for food security in the developing world are profound. There is no distinction within GATT proposals between subsidies used in the developed world to sustain over-production and those in the developing countries to encourage greater food self-reliance. Nigeria, for example, is threatened by trade sanctions as a result of its restriction on US wheat imports, introduced to try to enhance local food production. It is also likely that price support systems for indigenous farmers will become illegal. It was through such incentives that small-scale farmers in Zimbabwe achieved a tripling of maize production in the early 1980s.

If these measures become operational, it is likely that, whilst the aid organizations emphasize the critical need to encourage food self-reliance in the developing countries, more and more farmers in these regions will become involved in the production of export crops at the expense of the environment, local rural enterprise and the food needs of local peoples. The benefits will fall to the developed world. A senior GATT negotiator referred to the notion that developing countries need to feed themselves as an anachronism in the light of the 'ready availability of US cereals'.

The proposals for further trade liberalization under the latest GATT Round may also have a very direct impact on the environment through the undermining of various environmental protection measures and standards already taken in both the developing and developed worlds. GATT and the World Bank are currently arguing that interference in trade flows to secure environmental objectives should be outlawed. If a country wishes to impose environmental and health standards on productive activities, such as including environmental costs in its prices, it does not have a right under GATT to impose those standards on other countries. Such countries therefore risk making their own production uncompetitive on a world market where goods produced under less environmentally friendly conditions will still be traded.

It is argued that GATT, more than any other international instrument or treaty, will determine progress towards sustainable environmental policies. International trade is the most significant dimension of global economic activity, and in many developing countries trade represents more than 50 per cent of GDP. To a large extent, therefore, the new GATT accord will determine patterns and processes of resource exploitation and will have a considerable impact on many of the world's most pressing environmental problems. The minimal effort, to date, to assess the environmental implications of international trade by such an influential organization as GATT; the continued dominance within its membership of representatives of the developed world and multi-national companies; and the lack of representation of consumer or environmental groups, are all characteristics to be decried in the name of sustainable development.

International debt and the environment

Foreign borrowing can be highly beneficial, but it also has its costs in terms of the repayment of loans along with the interest accumulated on these. In recent years, these costs have tended to outweigh the benefits for developing countries. In the favourable global economic climate of the mid-1970s (declining real oil prices as a result of inflation, low interest rates and buoyant world trade), heavy borrowing enabled the developing countries to achieve relatively high growth rates whilst still being able to service their debts. The benefit at the time to the developed countries was a dampening of the recession owing to increased export demand on the part of the developing world. The finance for such a situation came from private international banks who acted to recycle the huge surplus of the oil exporters.

In the early 1980s, however, this favourable situation was reversed, primarily as a result of the second oil price rises of 1979. Import prices and interest rates rose, whereas export levels and primary commodity prices, in particular, fell very dramatically. Between 1970 and 1989, the external debt of the developing nations grew by over 1800 per cent from US$68.4 billion to US$1,283 billion. Burgeoning interest rates and the accumulation of debt from the previous decade combined to produce huge debt-servicing obligations for most developing countries. In response, many 'chose' to borrow even more heavily in the 1980s. However, private lending also slowed very dramatically in the 1980s, such that, by 1986, the developing countries were paying back US$30.7 billion more to the commercial and multilateral banks than they were receiving in new loans.

This debt crisis has two major implications for the prospects of sustainable development in the indebted nations. The need to increase short-term productivity puts pressure on countries to overexploit their natural resources, which in the long term raises the costs of correcting the environmental destruction inflicted now and reduces the potential for sustainable development of resources such as agriculture and forestry. In addition, the level of government austerity necessitated by debt servicing reduces a government's capacity to deal with environmental protection and rehabilitation.

The realization worldwide that developing countries cannot pay their external debts has led to numerous proposals for relieving and/or renegotiating the debts of these countries. Case study H highlights one attempt to address the adverse effects of debt on the environment very directly through what have been termed 'debt-for-nature swaps'. This is a concept designed to bring together the financiers handling the developing world's debts and conservationists.

Case study H

Debt-for-nature swaps

Trading of the developing countries' debt on the secondary market is not a new phenomenon. Several hundred million dollars' worth of debt changes hands daily as lending institutions sell off debts at a discount price to buyers who specialize in the collection of debt. The lender thereby recoups a proportion of the debt, but the buyer aims to recover something nearer to the full amount, and therefore make a profit. What is new, however, is that rather than solely big brokers being involved in the debt market, since 1987 a number of NGOs have, with very specific intentions, purchased a small proportion of a developing country's debt. The NGO, having purchased through voluntary donations a few million dollars' worth (say) of commercial bank debt, offers the debtor country a reprieve from that portion of debt in exchange for a commitment to a particular environmental project in the country. Another incentive to the debtor nations is that these projects can be paid for in local currency rather than foreign exchange.

The first ever 'debt-for-nature swap' took place in 1987, in which Conservation International paid $100,000 for $650,000 of

Case study H *(continued)*

Bolivian debt and forgave it in return for the equivalent of $250,000 in local currency as funds towards the Beri Biosphere Reserve. Although the amount of foreign debt relieved in this way is relatively small, commitment to the idea is mounting as is the number of projects and the number of agencies and institutions involved in these schemes. For example, no longer is it solely NGOs who are active in debt-for-nature projects. In March 1991, the Inter-American Development Bank announced its intention to institute such swaps in Mexico.

The success of future debt-for-nature swaps will rest on at least two key issues. First, the benefits of conservation are long term. It is extremely unlikely that NGOs, multilateral banks or individual governments will be able or willing to fund such projects to a level equivalent to the earnings which could accrue from the exploitation of that resource over the short term. The logging of the trees in the Beri Biosphere Reserve, for example, would undoubtedly earn a lot more than the amount of debt reduction enabled by the debt-for-nature scheme. There is therefore a moral question of such an attempt at long-term conservation in the light of unfulfilled short-term needs. Conservation under debt-for-nature swaps must ensure that benefits accrue to the people and such people must have very clearly perceived self-interest in the project.

Second, there is a danger that priorities in resource use within the developing countries will be set by outsiders, prompting fears of neo-colonialism on behalf of the debtor nations. There is evidence that the developing countries are becoming more receptive to debt-for-nature swaps. For example, Brazil had previously regarded such proposals as foreign meddling in the internal and environmental problems of the country. However, a change of President heralded $100 million of proposed swaps in Brazil in 1991.

National action

The UK government was the first to issue a formal response to the challenge of sustainable development as identified by the WCED. Other governments, such as those of the Scandinavian countries, Holland and

Japan, followed. By 1989, 22 countries and the EC had responded to the WCED with details of their progress towards the achievement of sustainable development policies. In addition, other countries from the developed nations, such as Australia and New Zealand, issued statements in the late 1980s on environmental issues. Many governments of the developing nations have also been involved in preparing action plans for the environment, often in cooperation with UN agencies and the World Bank. In Africa, for example, eight states had prepared National Environmental Action Plans by 1991. All such responses recognized the challenge of translating the theory of sustainable development into the reality of government programmes.

Figure 3.4 highlights the major elements of the Dutch national environmental policy plan. This was published in 1989 in response to the findings of the WCED and is referred to by Starke (1990) as containing 'some of the strongest language seen in an official document on the environment'.

Many national governments have also taken important actions with respect to specific components of the global environment since the

Plate 3.2 Recycling, Amsterdam
Source: Gordon Walker, Staffordshire University

Figure 3.4 Government of The Netherlands: National Environmental Policy Plan 1989, target areas for action

Agriculture:

- 70 per cent reduction in ammonia emissions;
- 50 per cent reduction in pesticide use.

Transport:

- Increased emphasis on public transport and bicycles;
- Emission ceilings, for nitrous oxide, hydrocarbons, carbon dioxide and noise, set for the years 2000 and 2010;
- Removal of tax perk for longer-distance car commuters;
- Preparation of 'kilometre reduction plans' by employers;
- Encouragement of freight transport by water and rail.

Physical planning:

- Aim to secure good public transport access to 'labour intensive' and 'visitor intensive' activities.

Industry:

- Acidifying and eutrophying substances to be cut by 50–75 per cent over 1985 levels by 2000.

Electricity and gas companies:

- Emission targets set for sulphur dioxide and nitrous oxide;
- Energy conservation strongly encouraged, particularly by energy distribution companies.

Building trade:

- Doubling of re-use of building and demolition waste by 2000;
- Securing 25 per cent improvement in energy conservation;
- Substitution of new materials for those with a serious environmental impact;
- Initiation of a 'sustainable building' project aimed at incorporating environmental objectives into construction works;
- Tightening of insulations standards for houses, offices and other buildings;
- Subsidy programme of 70 million Dutch Guilders per year for the insulation of existing houses.

Consumers:

- By 2000, all used batteries, tin, glass and paper to be collected separately for recycling;
- Electricity consumption to be stabilized at 1985 levels;
- Growth in passenger kilometres per car to be limited.

publication of *Our Common Future*. For example, many have undertaken to reduce the emissions of various substances within their borders. In 1989, President Bush announced the first overhaul of the US Clean Air Act for twenty years, which included cutting sulphur dioxide emissions by 50 per cent by the year 2000. Other governments, such as that of Brazil, are taking steps to halt the pace of rainforest destruction through the creation of reserve areas and the freezing of subsidies for mining and lumber companies in the Amazon basin. In Australia, soil erosion is one of the specific environmental issues which the government has addressed; 1990 was declared the Year of Landcare in that country, and a ten-year programme to introduce conservation programmes to stem soil erosion was initiated.

The pace of change by governments is uneven, however. There is evidence to suggest that there may be a new game of 'one-upmanship' amongst some national governments, to be the first to take the strongest action, such as on emissions. For example, in April 1989, the Norwegian government established the goal of freezing carbon dioxide output during the 1990s. Five months later, the Dutch government went further, pledging to freeze emissions by the middle of the decade. Such developments could be good for the environment, but it should not divert attention away from the actions of nations elsewhere, particularly in the developing world, whose capacity to engage in such a race may well be hampered precisely by those factors identified at the beginning of the chapter.

Non-Governmental Organizations and sustainable development

NGOs are highly diverse organizations, are engaged in various activities and operate at a variety of scales. They are not able to sign treaties, pass legislation or set targets for emissions as governments are able to. However, they are able to lobby for such actions to be taken, and have become an increasingly powerful force in the modification of governmental activities over the last twenty years. Increasingly, NGOs also have a role in an advisory capacity not just with governments but with business and international institutions. They are also involved in the implementation of projects, both on behalf of others and on their own initiatives.

The WCED recognized the key role which NGOs could have in fostering sustainable development based on their proven ability to secure popular participation in decision-making. In the developed world, NGOs have a long history of informing government decisions and lobbying for specific actions. As such, they have been influential in bringing the concerns of local people to the attention of national governments. There are now also an increasing number of NGOs in the developing world which are starting to open and deepen such channels of communication in these regions. In addition, those NGOs which operate internationally have much to contribute towards effecting sustainable development in practice through acting as sources of advice, as watchdogs on the activities of governments and through carrying out services which perhaps governments themselves are unable to.

The most significant development in terms of actions taken towards sustainable development may lie in the expanding role of NGOs, the growing number of them and the gains in official recognition of them over the last twenty years. The precise number of NGOs operating is unknown. However, it is recognized that, to promote sustainable development, there is a need to coordinate the rather fragmented activities of various conservation, development, relief or women's organizations. As a result, a number of coalitions for NGOs have been established. The intention of such networks as the African NGOs Environment Network (ANEN), the Asian NGO Coalition for Agrarian Reform and Rural Development (ANGOC) and the Environment Liaison Centre International (ELCI) is to help individual NGOs to see the connections between their own concerns and their common endeavour of sustainable human progress. For example, ECLI, the leading coalition of NGOs which is based in Nairobi, is in contact with more than 8,000 NGOs around the world.

The actions and achievements of particular NGOs are clearly diverse. The activities of international organizations such as Greenpeace are well known; these include action to stop whaling, efforts to ban shipments of hazardous waste and demonstrations against nuclear testing. The actions of NGOs in the developing countries are less well publicized. An exception is the Green Belt Movement of Kenya, which has received attention for its outstanding success and the commitment of its central campaigner, Professor Maathai. This project of tree planting started with a single nursery at a primary school in 1977 and spread to include 670 community nurseries and 20,000 private 'mini-Green Belts' by 1989. Professor Maathai has received many awards for the campaigning which she has done for both women's rights and the environment and she was chosen by the international community of NGOs to represent them at the Earth Summit. In Chapters 5 and 6, the role of selected NGOs in fostering sustainable development in the rural and urban sectors respectively are highlighted.

Conclusion

Many of the actions taken at various levels to promote sustainable development give cause for optimism. The major challenge to international institutions in the 1990s is to translate their rhetorical commitment for sustainable development into meaningful actions. Primarily, such actions must be directed at ending poverty and stimulating the growth of developing countries while giving greater weight to environmental concerns. The WCED suggests that this requires global economic growth to be revitalized; a commitment to the satisfactory workings of multilateral institutions; the negotiation of and adherence to international rules for trade which will allow freer access to markets for the products of the developing countries; a commitment to lower interest rates and to facilitate greater technology and capital flows to the developing countries.

Susbstantial optimism for further progress was expressed for the UNCED conference in Rio de Janeiro in 1992 at which representatives of multilateral institutions, national governments and NGOs all participated. Much of the post-summit analysis, however, has been pessimistic. This has tended to focus, for example, on the governments who refused to sign documents and on the contentious clauses within Agenda 21 (the comprehensive plan set out in advance of the summit to guide action for sustainable development in the future). However, it may be too soon to assess the lasting impacts of the Earth Summit. As seen with the 1972 UN Conference on the Human Environment, it is often the subsequent meetings/conferences/actions that such large meetings spawn which are the most significant. What is certain is that, if global environmental deterioration is to be halted, international cooperation and dialogue must occur in areas where national interests may not necessarily coincide, and NGOs must continue to act as watchdogs for such progress as well as to take their own actions.

Key ideas

1 Taking action towards sustainable development requires the reconciliation of key questions of responsibility, the power to respond and sovereignty.

2 International action towards sustainable development has been started in the key areas of trade, aid and international debt. Both donors and recipients of aid are now more aware of the need for environmentally sustainable projects.

3 Moves towards trade liberalization may have a number of direct and indirect negative effects on the environment, particularly in the developing world.

4 Debt servicing puts pressure on developing countries to overexploit natural resources in the short term, reduces the potential for sustainable development of resources in the future and reduces a government's capacity to deal with environmental protection and rehabilitation.

5 Many national governments have issued official responses to the WCED report and others have taken action on specific environmental problems raised by the Commission.

6 NGOs are thought to be the key to sustainable development in the future on the basis of their ability to mobilize local communities.

4
Sustainable rural livelihoods

In Chapter 2, reference was made to some of the linkages between poverty and the environment in both rural and urban areas. A vicious circle was identified in which people, because of their poverty, degrade the marginal environments in which they live even further because of a lack of alternative sustainable options. Some of the environmental effects of poverty include deforestation, desertification and the settlement of ecologically hazardous areas. The environments that the poor occupy have, in turn, characteristics such as declining land productivity, ill health, inadequate shelter and low levels of income.

For the large numbers of people resident in the developing world, their basic needs in terms of both development and conservation are immediate and local; survival in the short term is their primary concern and for this they depend largely on the resources of the surrounding area. For approximately 70 per cent of the people living in the developing world, these needs are also rurally based. Although levels of urbanization in the developing world are predicted to increase, it is also certain that the absolute numbers resident in rural areas are rising and will continue to do so under projected population increases. Providing sustainable rural livelihoods, not just for the present population but for many billions more, is therefore an urgent endeavour, as these populations will have to be supported on what is often a very fragile and difficult environment.

This chapter identifies the characteristics of rural livelihoods in the developing world, the major sources of change within these systems and the conditions and characteristics of sustainable rural development.

The rural environment

Agriculture and rural livelihoods

Livelihood is defined as adequate stocks and flows of food and cash to meet basic needs. For the majority of rural households, these stocks are met through agricultural production, although as Dixon (in this series)

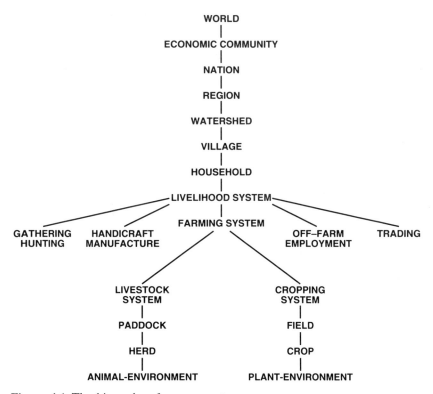

Figure 4.1 The hierarchy of agroecosystems
Source: Conway, G. R. (1987) 'The properties of agroecosystems', *Agricultural Systems* 24 (2): 95–117.

has shown, non-agricultural incomes may also be important at particular times. Figure 4.1 illustrates a number of sources of food or cash outside agricultural production which may be secured for individual livelihoods. It also shows how agricultural production itself may be based primarily on the management of crops or animals. Despite the importance of these alternative sources of income for rural households, Chambers (1983), for example, is certain that 'for adequate and decent livelihoods that are sustainable, much depends on policies which affect agriculture'.

Plate 4.1 Brick making as a source of rural income, Zimbabwe
Source: Author

As seen in Chapter 3, however, few societies now function in isolation from other peoples and places. Figure 4.1 shows how individual rural livelihood systems are connected into a wider hierarchy of 'agroeco-systems' which extends ultimately to a world level. The specific features of an individual system are shaped by both the physical and human environments. For example, the nature of agricultural production and the participation in and importance of non-agricultural activities will vary not only with the physical characteristics of the location, such as soils and climate, but also according to socio-economic and political factors operating at all levels in this hierarchy.

Rural livelihood systems are also under constant change. For example, a decline in demand for a particular handicraft item such as basketry (an economic factor) or a lack of rainfall (an environmental factor) may operate at the local level to prompt change in individual livelihoods. Further up the hierarchy, a new national government policy concerning recommended soil conservation practices may also serve to change local cropping patterns. The number of potential factors shaping individual rural livelihood systems is limitless; the impact may be direct or indirect, large or small, immediate or delayed. The current form of rural livilihood systems in the developing world is the outcome of all of these factors over time. It is the interdependence of all elements within the widest world agroecosystem that ensures that any change (whether climatic, economic, social or political) will have implications for the operation of systems at all other levels. This constitutes the challenge for future sustainable rural development.

Systems under change

Despite the range of factors for change in rural livelihood systems and their varying impact according to the specifics of the human and physical environments in any location at a particular time, there have been attempts to model what has been termed the 'agrarian transformation' for various parts of the world. For example, there are common characteristics in the way in which societies changed in Europe from an agricultural to an industrial base. This change was from largely peasant production (small-scale subsistence agriculture carried out by people who are both workers and owners of at least some of the resources they use) to often large-scale, specialized, non-agricultural activities based in urban locations. These transformations occurred in the now advanced capitalist countries of the world and have become the accepted characteristics of economic development.

In contrast, the developing world has experienced a partial or 'retarded' agrarian transformation as a result of its incorporation into the world economy. In continuity with the situation in nineteenth-century Europe, commercialization of rural economies in the developing world has occurred. Land and labour now have à monetary value and people have to sell some of what they produce and buy some of their household requirements. As a result, some people in the developing world have been able to make profits, expand their operations and move into non-agricultural activities. However, large numbers of rural people in the developing world remain in peasant production with very few material assets or specialized skills. Both the relationships between people and between people and the environment have changed dramatically. Case study I highlights the impact of such a partial transformation of rural society with respect to the ability of rural households to cope with drought and resultant food insecurity.

Case study I

The decline of indigenous coping strategies for drought

> If you change a man's way of life, you had better have something of value with which to replace it.
>
> (Kikuyu proverb)

Drought is not a new phenomenon in many areas of the world. What is new is the level of suffering with which drought has been associated in the latter part of this century, particularly in the developing world. Drought is not a sufficient condition for famine, but it is often the final trigger for large-scale starvation and death. Since drought has undoubtedly been an important factor around which rural communities in the developing world have had to adjust their activities for many centuries, research is now focused increasingly on understanding why it is only recently that people, in such large numbers, have been unable to cope with drought.

Such research has shown that there are many adjustments that individuals and communities can and do make to reduce the impact of drought on their food supply. Some of these 'coping strategies' involve modifications of their relationship with the environment, others require adjustments in their political, economic and social circumstances. For example, detailed knowledge of variations in the local ecology (including soils, topography and micro-climate), combined with careful selection, siting and mixture of crops, would enable the best use of available resources and offer a degree of security against the failure of any one crop. Economic coping strategies would include various responses to drought, such as selling off livestock, but also measures to prevent hardship, such as storage of crops from good seasons or

Case study I *(continued)*

accumulating savings through agricultural or supplementary sources.

There are also a number of social strategies to which people turn in times of hardship and which help to lessen the impact of drought. These may operate at a variety of levels in the social system and are based on individual or household membership of institutions such as family and clan. Assistance may be found through these institutions in terms of gifts of food, loans of cash or even the temporary support of members of one household within another. Such assistance between members of communities is usually based on reciprocity; it may represent repayment of past kindness or a commitment to help in the future.

Such coping strategies amongst communities living in harsh environments have developed over many years and evidence suggests that additional strategies are evolving as the physical, political–economic and social environments change for these people. Several authors suggest, however, that survival is being bought at the price of intensified integration into the market system. Watts (1983), for example, identified the 'colonial triad' of taxes, cash crops and monetization as central factors in the decreased subsistence security of small peasant households in the developing world. He argues that the introduction and entrenchment of these three factors into rural economies, starting with the colonial period, has led to a breakdown in the 'moral economy' of such societies.

The explanation within such analyses for the increased hardship that is prompted by drought, which is expressed in the large-scale death through starvation that has been seen over the last two decades particularly in Africa, lies in the 'retarded transformation' of these economies. The problem is that the breakdown of traditional coping strategies has left large numbers of people increasingly vulnerable not just to natural events, such as climatic drought, but also to crises associated with their incorporation into the market economy, such as the fluctuations in cash crop prices. Whilst one set of values, which had regulated successfully the relationship between people and the environment, has been eroded, another effective set has yet to be incorporated.

Marginality and resource-poor farmers

The WCED identified three crude types of contemporary agriculture across the globe; 'industrial' (largely confined to the industrialized world but also in specialized enclaves in the developing world), 'green revolution' agriculture (in areas of the developing world characterized by reliable rainfall or irrigation technologies) and 'resource-poor' agriculture (found throughout the developing world).

It is estimated that one-quarter of the world's population are dependent on this third type of agriculture for their livelihoods; they are amongst the world's poorest people and they live in the world's most highly vulnerable ecological areas. It is therefore in these areas that the major challenges to sustainable rural development lie.

> Poverty and environmental destruction are becoming inseparable twins, less because the absolute numbers of people have grown than because the poorest people (who have the least access to investment capital and technology) occupy the lands that need the most infrastructure, management, and external inputs if their utilization is not to result in land degradation and environmental destruction.
>
> (Leonard *et al.* 1989)

It is with respect to the poverty identified by Leonard, in terms of both the human and physical environments, that resource-poor farmers are commonly referred to as 'marginal'. In ecological terms, not only are such farmers concentrated in the most fragile areas, such as those prone to flooding and adverse climatic conditions, but their land use activities, such as the burning of forest resources for fuel, are threatening the ecological stability of such regions even further. In economic terms, many such farmers are utilizing lands of a quality, and at an intensity of production, at which returns on their labour do not exceed the costs. Many farmers find themselves in a downward spiral of borrowing money or resources to feed themselves or to cover their costs of production in the off-season, only to have to pay these back at unfavourable rates and times in the successive season.

Such farmers are also referred to as marginal in a political sense; they are often uninformed, disorganized and outside any formal political system. They may also have very little political power in terms of their participation in decision-making or control over the many structures which influence their daily lives, such as local administration or the operation of the markets.

The causes of such marginality are diverse and specific to particular places and times, as identified above. High population growth rates and the relatively low demand for labour created by the capital-intensive nature of industrialization which has occurred in the developing world are certainly part of the explanation. The effects are more uniform. For example, these farmers, because of their economic position, lack the financial resources to invest in the capital equipment or inputs necessary to raise production or to implement the land use management techniques appropriate to the physical ecology of these areas. As a result of their political and ecological marginality (as well as their spatial remoteness), they often do not receive the benefits of public investment in services or infrastructure that is necessary to the success of modern agriculture.

It is, however, to the aspect of technology that attention within rural research and development has shifted over the last ten years. Research into the complexity of farming systems in the developing world, together with a better understanding of the decisions which face resource-poor farmers, has led to a re-evaluation of the priorities within agricultural research and the recommendations for action which stem from these. It is now appreciated more widely that rarely do farmers fail, through ignorance, to effect land use decisions which will raise productivity or conserve resources. Rather their behaviour is, more regularly, rational in the light of their political-economic, social and environmental circumstances.

There is now an awareness on behalf of development 'professionals' (both academics and practitioners) of the need to complement 'normal' research and extension activities with an approach which starts with the knowledge, problems and priorities of farmers themselves. This approach has been termed 'Farmer First'. Case study J highlights the origins and value of this complementary approach to research and development of resource-poor agriculture. Work which has adopted this complementary approach has, to date, shown the greatest progress towards implementing sustainable rural development in practice.

Case study J

The value of indigenous technologies

Rural people's knowledge and scientific knowledge are complementary in their strengths and weaknesses. Combined they may achieve what neither would alone.

(Chambers 1983)

Case study J *(continued)*

An anthropologist at the International Rice Research Institute in the Philippines (an organization central to the promotion of the 'green revolution' technologies) concluded recently that 90 per cent of the technologies being promoted from that institute had been derived from the ideas of farmers themselves. Yet there is still substantial scepticism about farmers' knowledge and their potential contribution in farming research development; rarely do farmers record their findings in writing or research papers, the conventional reference point for scientists. As a result, it has been suggested that the 'history of agriculture is written without reference to the main innovators in the long-term process of technological change'.

In contrast, during the 1950s and 1960s, there was tremendous optimism for the role of western science in raising agricultural production throughout the world. The success at the time of the green revolution in India contributed to this faith in western technology. The concern was for transferring the new technology to other parts of the developing world. However, when farmers were unable to gain yields on their own farms comparable to those achieved at experimental stations, research became focused on the constraints within local farming systems.

It is now thought that research conducted at experimental stations has limitations for solving the 'real-life' problems of the farmer (particularly the resource-poor farmer). Scientists have an important role to play in conducting research *about* a problem, for example, how potatoes grow. But for *solving* a problem, such as how to grow potatoes, it is thought that farmers in fact have a lot to teach scientists. The problem for research and extension activities, therefore, becomes not how to transfer technology from research station to farmer but how to close the gap between the two so that insights from both can be shared and built upon.

The value of indigenous technology and the benefits of closer links between scientist and farmer can be seen in the example of a technology for potato storage. The credit for the successful spread in Peru of a new technique for storing potatoes (known as diffused light storage) is usually given to the research staff of the International Potato Centre in that country. In fact, it was a

Case study J *(continued)*

technique first observed by scientists amongst indigenous farmers which was then tested and refined in the experimental station at the Centre. The idea was then passed back to the farmers.

However, an investigation into the uptake of the technique found that only in 2 per cent of 4,000 cases was this technology adopted according to the recommendations of the extension agents. More regularly, farmers experimented themselves with the technology; they first took a handful of tubers and compared shrinkage and sprout elongation for those kept in the light with those stored under the old practices in darkness. Farmers selected elements of the recommended technology to suit their own constantly changing circumstances. Financial considerations played a part in the selection of elements, most beginning with small quantities before moving on to larger investments, but so did social factors, such as the prevention of theft.

It can been seen from this example that it is not possible to distinguish between indigenous and western technology. They are complementary and mutually reinforcing. Similarly, the distinction between adoption and non-adoption is misleading. The challenges, however, of supporting farmer innovation and of building on farmer–researcher interactions are not to be underestimated. The locus of research has to change from research station to the farmers' fields, where the farmers become the central experimenters. It has implications for extension agents too; their role should be to help farmers adapt rather than to hand down technology from above. The alternative is for the gap to remain and for the 'blame', in terms of limited success in solving farmers' problems, to continue to be passed between 'ignorant farmers' and the 'poor extension services'.

Towards sustainable rural development

Conditions for change

The limits to or constraints on sustainable development (rural or urban) can be termed both natural and structural. With respect to agricultural development, there are natural limits to maintaining resource productivity over time, for example, those set by the physical characteristics of soils to regenerate fertility, even with the aid of chemical fertilizers. In addition, it has been seen that the power of individuals to implement certain land use decisions at the local level is in part determined by a whole set of political, economic and social factors. For example, market prices are a primary influence on farmers' decisions over which crops to grow.

It is individuals who hold the key to sustainable resource-using practices, whether urban or rurally based; they ultimately decide how resources are to be used. As seen in the case of resource-poor farmers, however, the range of options which individual land users have at their disposal will depend very closely on their financial resources, external inputs, access to technology and even their political power. However, it is suggested that even the poorest farmers do have options. Chambers (1983) has observed that

> individual behaviour is not fully determined. Political, social and economic forces do operate but, when they are dissected, sooner or later we come to individual people who are acting, feeling and perceiving. All are to some degree capable of changing what they do. The sum of small actions make great movements.

The concept of the agroecosystem was used above to highlight that the structural limits which affect individual farming practices operate at a variety of levels. A number of conditions for sustainable agricultural development in the future can therefore be identified as follows.

At the international level, there are several key factors which may inhibit the achievement of sustainable agricultural development within the developing countries. Some of these were identified in Chapter 4. Many of the developing countries have a high dependence on one or two agricultural commodities for export, yet prices for these on the world markets have been declining since the 1950s. Factors such as the subsidizing by the USA and the EC of their own agricultural exports and the price support given to farmers within such regions have been important in raising production but also in lowering world prices. Protectionism on behalf of the developed countries, through import restrictions on agricultural goods, has also served to discriminate against producers in the developing world. The consequent vulnerability of developing world economies within agricultural markets is a serious constraint on the prospects for sustainable development. This vulnerability is also being entrenched by the World Bank's encouragement of developing countries to expand export commodities further in order to service debts.

However, the impact of these international level constraints on a particular developing nation and the prospects for sustainable development in specific regions of such countries will, to an extent, depend on national policies. Although government policy is a product of a very complex set of factors, key issues in determining the prospects for sustainable agricultural development will include the financial commitment to export or food-crop production, to large versus small-scale farming and to favoured or resource-poor farmers. Although no single form or scale of production is inherently more or less sustainable than another, past emphases on the large-scale production of export crops in the more favoured locations of the developing world has been shown to be unsustainable in terms of not only the practices employed but also the people it excluded. A major difficulty at all scales is that the problems of natural resource management within agricultural production have not, to date, been considered adequately.

Although there are a large number of ways in which government policy may influence agricultural production either directly or indirectly, most developing world economies are characterized by active government intervention in markets, and therefore pricing policies are likely to play a very important role in determining the prospects for sustainable agricultural development. Farmers are unlikely to conserve resources if there are powerful economic incentives driving them in the other direction. Policies regarding exchange rates, food prices, subsidies and the activities of marketing boards all have an impact on the prices of agricultural goods to the consumer and the prices paid to the producer, for example.

But it is at the local level that some of the most profound changes will have to occur. In Chapter 1, it was noted that the theoretical necessity of focusing development at the poorest sectors of society had been recognized; the interdependence of environment and development was widely appreciated and a focus on the welfare needs of the poor was required if the goals of either future development or conservation of the environment were to be achieved. The challenge of effecting these commitments in practice is still a relatively new endeavour. However, there are sufficient examples of successful local rural projects, which appear to be sustainable, to make suggestions as to the primary characteristics of such projects if they are to be shared elsewhere.

The characteristics of success

Five major prerequisites for successful sustainable rural development have been put forward, based on recent experience:

1 A learning-process approach;
2 People's priorities first;
3 Secure rights and gains;
4 Sustainability through self-help;
5 Staff calibre, commitment and continuity.

The first prerequisite is in contrast to the 'blueprint' approach which has characterized many development projects in the past. Rather than holding to a rigid set of aims and procedures, projects which have been sustainable are continually modified during the course of the project. Changes are made in response to dialogue between all interested parties and the experience gained during the course of the operation of the project. Successful projects also identified and responded to people's perceived needs in the local area. Too often in the past, 'outsiders' (not simply international advisers but also the urban-based policy makers of the country) have assumed that they knew what poor people wanted when, in fact, the priorities of the different groups would vary quite widely. Putting the priorities of individual land users and communities first is therefore the second prerequisite for sustainable rural development.

The third lesson for sustainable rural development is based on the need to take a long-term view of resource use. People will not take a long-term view of resource use if they do not have secure rights to those resources and the gains from them. When people are sure, for example, that they have the rights to the products from trees that they plant, invest in and manage, they plant many more than they do when there are restrictions on the use or appropriation of such resources. People's perceived self-interest in a project is fundamental for ensuring their sustained participation and it is suggested that, except in the case of deeply impoverished peoples, participation should be entirely voluntary and without any form of inducement or subsidy. When people partici-pate for the sole reason that they have seen success achieved and have become enthusiastic enough to work towards achieving it for themselves, projects tend to be more relevant, to spread more quickly and to encourage innovation on the part of the people. A self-help approach aids the sustainability of not only the existing project but also those of the future.

The achievement of all four of the above prerequisites for sustainable rural development depends on the qualities of the staff of the project; their competence, dedication and involvement over substantial periods. It was found that short-term, poorly motivated and insensitive staff, for example, were unable to develop the relationships with local peoples that were required for sustainability.

Case study K highlights the particular characteristics of the Yatenga Soil and Water Conservation project in Burkina Faso which were important to its success and sustainability.

Case study K

country in north western Africa.

Soil and water conservation in Yatenga, Burkina Faso

The Yatenga region of Burkina Faso is a heavily populated area in which the average area cultivated per person is as low as 0.5 hectares and livestock pressures on the limited grazing area has led to extensive degradation of soils and vegetation. There is little opportunity to extend the cultivated or grazed areas such that land improvement is the only future for the livelihood system in the region.

In 1979, a forestry project was started in the area, but the commitment of the local peoples to planting trees was low and the survival of the trees was inhibited by the activities of stock under the high pressure for grazing resources. In response to the villagers' evident preference for conserving soil and water rather than planting trees, the project was modified towards the testing of soil and water conservation techniques on farmers' fields. A key to the subsequent success of the modified project was the development of a simple technology for determining the slope of the land and therefore the location of contour lines for the construction of the rock bunds which were the essential means through which water was to be 'harvested'.

The use of rock bunds to collect runoff during the rains, rather than earth bunds which had previously been suggested, was in response to the priorities identified by the farmers themselves. It was a key factor in the sustainability of the project. In conditions of low and erratic rainfall, the farmers' priority was to keep water on their fields rather than to control the movement of water across

Case study K *(continued)*

their fields. They preferred rock bunds to earth bunds for several reasons: rock bunds are not damaged by runoff and therefore this reduces maintenance; they are permeable, so that crops and therefore yields can be increased; they encourage the infiltration of water, so raising the effectiveness of the limited rainfall in the area.

The increased adoption of bunding, in conjunction with the use of organic manures and improved tillage methods, has led to the reclamation of degraded and abandoned lands in the region, so enabling the expansion of the cultivated area. Yields were found to increase impressively in the short term, which encouraged more and more farmers to adopt the technology. The number of hectares with bunds doubled every year from 1983 and had reached 1,300 hectares in 1986. Farmers attended first to their individual fields and the project provided them with material support in the form of shovels and wheelbarrows. There was also a small revolving stock of maize flour which was made available to farmers within participating groups and which could be used by individuals to prepare food for those who helped them in bund construction on their private fields.

Farmer training focused on the use of the level to establish the lie of the land, the importance of respecting contour lines, practical sessions in rock bund construction and the organization of the treatment of individual and communal fields. The project was successful because it was farmer-oriented in its approach; the techniques were essentially improved traditional practices. The project was modified in accordance with priorities set by the farmers themselves and local participation was solely on the basis of the farmers' perceived self-interest in the improvements to their farming system that were enabled by the project.

Women and the environment

It has been suggested that women may have a key role in promoting sustainable development in the developing world. Momsen (in this series) has highlighted the role that women play in the spheres of both production and reproduction. As producers of food and other goods to

Plate 4.2 Women do men's work
Source: Mike Kesby, Keele University

gain income for the household and through their role in caring for the family, women are dependent directly on a healthy environment in order to carry out these functions. In many parts of the developing world, it is women who are the collectors and managers of agricultural produce, water, forestry and energy resources. In conditions of environmental decline, as evidenced by soil erosion, drought and deforestation, for example, it is largely women who suffer an increased burden in the difficulty of maintaining their productive and reproductive activities.

There are several reasons why it is suggested that projects to address the major environmental and development challenges in the rural sector of the developing world should work with women to achieve sustainability. One reason is that women are already, in many areas, the main environmental managers and so they have the knowledge to build on concerning local environments and the constraints and opportunities that they present for sustainable development. By not acknowledging women's existing role as conservationists, governments and international agencies risk losing valuable allies in the fight to conserve the environment.

Plate 4.3 The collection of energy resources, Zimbabwe
Source: Author

Women are also known to work together well. Some of the most successful examples of sustainable development to date have been built on women's initiatives. For example, the Chipko movement in India started with a small group of women presenting non-violent resistance to the contract felling of trees in their local area. The principles and practices of this original group have since spread to hundreds of local autonomous initiatives for the protection of forests. In addition, women are the carers of children and therefore will have a strong influence on changing attitudes to the environment over both the short term and the long.

Supporting women in conservation will also lead to improvements in their status, which will enhance their ability to participate in future development activities. Women do need such support; their full integration into the development process as both agents and beneficiaries will depend on their equitable access to land, credit, education, health and training. Improvements in women's status and conservation of the environment are suggested to be mutually reinforcing goals. One observer notes that 'there can be no liberation for women and no solution to the ecological crisis within a society whose fundamental model of relationships continues to be one of domination.'

Conclusion

For too long, the debates about both the environment and development have been dominated by the interests and values of the rich rather than the poor, men rather than women, and urban rather than rural. The results of this emphasis have been seen in this chapter: deteriorating environments, rising poverty and the increasing concentration of resource-poor farmers in some of the most ecologically fragile areas of the world. Reversing these priorities is an essential precondition for sustainable rural development in the future and some of the achievements in this direction have been detailed.

Making the rural poor the starting point in research and development has been seen to have benefits for the environment and development. These are likely to go on accruing in the future as people gain control over their own resources, have more options regarding resource use and acquire security in their agricultural and non-agricultural activities. The long-term benefits of providing secure rural livelihoods for the rural poor will also fall to the wider communities; rural insecurity is a major factor in maintaining high fertility rates and in prompting rural to urban migration. Thus, improving rural livelihood security will help to relieve population pressure on resources (a central prerequisite for sustainable development in the future) as well as to slow the demand for employment and shelter in urban areas, which are currently two key demands on the limited financial resources for urban planning in the developing world.

Key ideas

1 For approximately 70 per cent of the population of the developing world, environmental concerns and development needs are focused on immediate survival, are local and are rurally based.
2 Agriculture remains the primary means through which rural people in the developing world meet their basic needs.
3 Rural livelihood systems throughout the world are under constant change.
4 Indigenous coping strategies for drought have been undermined but

not replaced as a result of the retarded transformation of peasant agriculture in the developing world.

5 Many farmers in the developing world are 'resource-poor' and 'marginal'. Technology for resource-poor farmers could be more effective if it combined rural people's knowledge and scientific knowledge.

6 Successful, sustainable rural development projects have shared a number of common characteristics. In particular, NGOs and women are considered to hold the key to future sustainable rural development projects.

5
Sustainable urban livelihoods

Global trends in urbanization

The world's economic system is increasingly becoming an urban one, as is its population. In 1800, only 3 per cent of the total world population lived in towns and cities. It is estimated that by 2000, this figure will have risen to approximately 50 per cent. There are certainly problems in making such predictions; detailed understanding of past changes is hampered by poor data coverage and quality, and acccurate distinctions between rural and urban populations continue to be elusive (see Drakakis-Smith in this series). However, it is clear that the pace and scale of change, in terms of urban patterns and processes throughout the globe, are substantially different today from any earlier period. The lack of historical precedent gives rise to a concern for human capacity to cope with this level of change and to forge future sustainable urban development.

Throughout history, cities have been built to serve a variety of functions; as forts, market places, and as centres of administration or industry. All cities have experienced periods of growth and decline and all tend to raise contradictory views concerning the nature and purpose of the city. Cities have been viewed variously as the centre of alienation, evil and immorality, and as the seat of intellect and the home for artistic and commercial innovation.

The variety of forces shaping urbanization and the complex and contradictory views concerning patterns and processes of urbanization continue today in both the developed and developing worlds. However, the WCED suggests that the future 'urban challenge' lies firmly in the developing world. Although the developed world is more urbanized in that a greater proportion of its national populations are resident in towns and cities, a greater proportion of the world's total population is resident in the towns and cities of the developing world. These cities are currently growing at rates above 3 per cent per annum, in contrast to the 0.5 per cent rates of growth common to the developed world. Table 5.1 shows the absolute growth in the urban populations of the world and the rising proportion of the total world population which is resident in the towns and cities of the developing world.

Table 5.1 Global urban population growth, 1950–90

	Urban population (millions)				
	1950	*1960*	*1970*	*1980*	*1990*
World total	734	1031	1371	1764	2234
More developed countries	447	571	698	798	877
Less developed countries (LDCs)	287	460	673	966	1357
LDCs as % of world total	39	45	49	55	61

Source: Adapted from *World Resources 1988–89*, World Resources Institute, Washington, DC.

Another major implication for future sustainable urban development is that urban growth within countries of the developing world is highly concentrated in one or two centres. In 34 developing countries, more than 40 per cent of the urban population is concentrated in one city, in many the proportion is over 60 per cent. Rates of urban growth in the developing world are also higher than for the growth of their populations as a whole. This is due not only to the large influx of migrants from rural areas to the cities but also to natural increase of urban populations (linked to their age structure). It is these patterns of urbanization in the developing world which are the concern of the WCED.

The processes of urban change in the developing world are also without historical precedent. In nineteenth-century Europe, people migrated to the towns and cities in search of employment and economic advancement. The industrial activities located in these areas depended on this process of migration to raise output and generate wealth. Urbanisation, industrialization and modernization (the adoption of urban values) were processes which occurred simultaneously in the cities of Europe and were mutually reinforcing. Currently in the developing world, urbanization is occurring independently from industrialization and modernization. In consequence, urban unemployment is very high. For example, even during the 1960s, a period of relatively rapid growth in manufacturing output in the developing countries, new industrial developments did not generate a sufficient number of employment opportunities to absorb the supply of labour. Table 5.2 illustrates how manufacturing output in the developing countries increased in this period without a corresponding increase in manufacturing employment. For example, Ethiopia experienced a 12.8 per cent increase in annual manufacturing output in the period 1963–9, but this level of growth was not matched by an equal expansion in job opportunities. In fact, employment growth was only 50 per cent of manufacturing growth (6.4 per cent annual increase).

In 1975, the World Bank estimated that there were three times as

Table 5.2 Industrialization and employment in developing countries, 1963–9

Region/countries	Manufacturing annual output growth (%)	Manufacturing employment growth (%)
AFRICA		
Ethiopia	12.8	6.4
Kenya	6.4	4.3
Nigeria	14.1	5.3
Egypt	11.2	0.7
ASIA		
India	5.9	5.3
Pakistan	12.3	2.6
Philippines	6.1	4.8
Thailand	10.7	−12.0
LATIN AMERICA		
Brazil	6.5	1.1
Colombia	5.9	2.8
Costa Rica	8.9	2.8
Dominican Republic	1.7	−3.3
Equador	11.4	6.0
Panama	12.9	7.4

Source: Todaro, M. P. (1989) *Economic Development in the Third World*, London: Longman.

many households in poverty in the rural areas of the developing world as there were in urban. However, the World Bank now predicts that this will be reversed by the turn of the century, because of the high rates of urbanization. In some cities of the developing world, over 50 per cent of residents are known to be below the poverty line. Urban poverty is a global phenomenon but, in the developing countries, the numbers of people living at or below subsistence levels are much larger and the resources available for reversing this situation much smaller than in the developed world.

Poor people in poor environments

In Chapter Two, it was seen that poverty is 'retreating' into particular geographical locations, often those of high ecological vulnerability. In the urban sector of the developing world, incomes tend to be higher than those in rural areas but sharp inequalities in the distribution of total income serve to maintain larger and larger numbers of urban people in poverty. The bottom 50 per cent of urban households regularly receive less than 25 per cent of the total income. Because of their poverty, many residents of cities in the developing world have no option but to live in environments which may be detrimental to their own well-being and to degrade the environments further in the course of securing their basic needs. In order to understand the challenge of sustainable urban development which this poverty–environment connection constitutes, it is necessary to elaborate further the characteristics of both the physical and human environments of cities in the developing world.

Low incomes

Few of the urban poor can afford to be unemployed for any length of time. Many, in fact, will be underemployed; either they are working less than they would like or are doing so at such low rates of production that their labour could be withdrawn with very little impact on overall output. The numbers of people underemployed in the cities of the developing world is even harder to assess accurately than the levels of open unemployment, although the former is likely to be several times higher than the latter. However, there is a close correlation between poverty and underemployment; in the main, those without regular employment or with only scattered part-time employment are also among the very poor.

Plate 5.1 Informal sector employment, Harare
Source: Author

In response to a lack of employment opportunities within the 'formal' sector, many urban residents in the developing world look to a wide variety of both legitimate and illegitimate income opportunities available within the 'informal' economy. Table 5.3 shows the estimated share of urban labour force in the informal sector for a number of cities in the developing world. Such activities commonly are small-scale in operation, rely on indigenous resources and skills acquired outside the formal schooling system, are labour-intensive and operate in un-regulated markets. The types of activities include retail distribution, small-scale transport, personal services (such as shoe-shining), security services, prostitution, begging and crime. A study of informal sector activities in Kano in northern Nigeria found a total of 6,665 enterprises in 52 types of activities, over 50 per cent of which involved trade.

Inferior housing

Housing costs are higher in urban areas than in rural and land for housing is also more scarce. In conditions of sharp contrasts and

Table 5.3 Estimated share of urban labour force in the informal sector in selected developing countries

Area	Share (%)
AFRICA	
Abidjan, Ivory Coast	31
Lagos, Nigeria	50
Kumasi, Ghana	60–70
Nairobi, Kenya	44
Urban areas, Senegal	50
Urban areas, Tunisia	34
ASIA	
Calcutta, India	40–50
Jakarta, Indonesia	45
Colombo, Sri Lanka	19
Singapore	23
Urban areas, Thailand	26
Urban areas, Pakistan	69
LATIN AMERICA	
Córdoba, Argentina	38
São Paulo, Brazil	43
Rio de Janeiro, Brazil	24
Urban areas, Chile	39
Bogotá, Colombia	43
Quito, Ecuador	48
Urban areas, Peru	60
Urban areas, Venezuela	44
Kingston, Jamaica	33

Source: Todaro, M. P. (1989) *Economic Development in the Third World*, London: Longman.

inequalities in wealth in cities of the developing world, residential segregation is increasing. Segregation is the process whereby those who can afford to pay more acquire the most desirable locations. Residential segregation reflects not only the inherent characteristics of the land (its height, soils, micro-climate, etc.) but also the acquired characteristics of the location, such as its infrastructure, servicing and amenity value. The urban poor are unable to afford preferred locations. In consequence, they tend to occupy the worst land in terms of both inherent and acquired characteristics.

There are at least three distinct types of poor urban dwellers in cities of the developing world: the homeless, those living in slums or tenements, and squatters occupying 'illegal' shanty-town developments. In India, more than half of the urban households occupy a single room, with an average occupancy per room of 4.4 persons. Many others are

Plate 5.2 Bangkok squatter settlement
Source: David Drakakis-Smith, Keele University

forced to sleep on the pavements at night. During the 1980s, just one formal housing unit was added to the total urban housing stock for every nine new households in the developing world. As a result, the majority of the urban population in such cities is being housed in unauthorized informal settlements.

High vulnerability to hazard

Wherever the urban poor in cities of the developing world are concentrated, it is commonly at high densities in areas of low rent. Low rents reflect the poverty of these environments and the consequent low demand for such locations from other commercial or residential uses. Regularly such locations are close to hazardous installations, such as chemical factories, and suffer continuous air and water pollution as well as the prospect of sudden fire or explosion. For example, as Gupta revealed (in this series), it was the high concentration of low income people around the Union Carbide Factory in Bhopal which caused so many to be killed or permanently injured (over 3,000 dead and approximately 100,000 seriously injured). Case study L highlights the interdependence of poverty and vulnerability to hazardous events such as earthquakes.

Case study L

Vulnerability to earthquake hazard and potential for disaster in Peru

Disasters are usually measured in terms of the large-scale loss of life, serious injury and destruction of resources/property. Disasters are the result not only of an environmental hazard event but also of human vulnerability.

Environmental hazards include both 'natural' hazards, such as earthquakes, and hazards of the 'human environment', such as the risk from dangerous industrial installations or flooding prompted

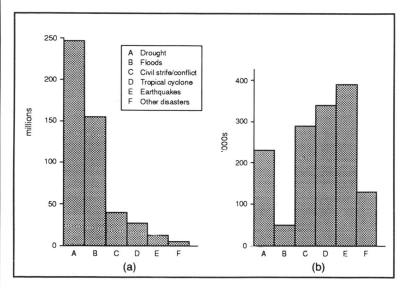

Figure 5.1 Numbers of people affected (a) and killed (b) by disasters, 1970–9

Source: Wijkman, A. and Timberlake, L. (1984) *Natural Disasters: Acts of God or Acts of Man?*, London: Earthscan.

Case study L *(continued)*

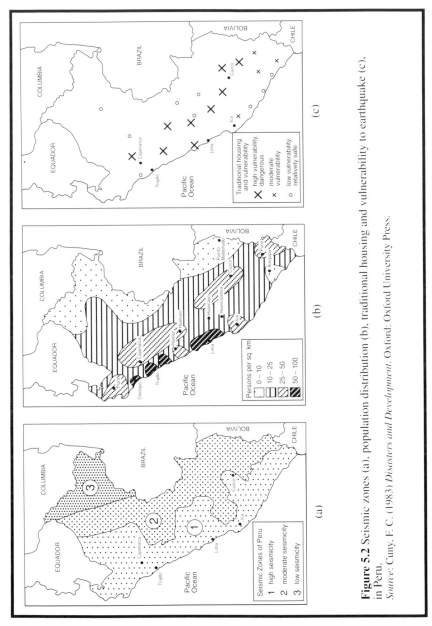

Figure 5.2 Seismic zones (a), population distribution (b), traditional housing and vulnerability to earthquake (c), in Peru.

Source: Cuny, F. C. (1983) *Disasters and Development.* Oxford: Oxford University Press.

Case study L *(continued)*

by human land-use practices. Human vulnerability to environmental hazards is a product of both geographical location (the physical exposure to the range of hazardous events which are likely to occur at a particular place) and human tolerance (a product of socio-economic circumstances which determine both where people live and how they live). Cannon has observed that the roots of human vulnerability to environmental hazards are the same as those of poverty itself, namely, control over resources and power both nationally and internationally.

It is the recognition of the role of poverty in creating human vulnerability to environmental hazards and the role of human agency in creating more hazardous environments that explains how both the number of disaster events recorded annually and the number of people affected or killed by such events are increasing (see Figure 5.1).

Peru is one of the most seismically active countries in the world; between 1970 and 1980, two major and several minor earthquakes struck the country. Figure 5.2a shows the locations of greatest seismic activity in Peru. Figure 5.2b shows the location of population in Peru and highlights the concentration of settlement in the coastal zones. Many of these people are highly vulnerable to the earthquakes because of their physical location.

One of the primary effects of seismic activity is a series of violent motions in the ground. People rarely die because the earth shakes, however; they die because the roof falls in. Internationally, building technology is in large measure available to prevent such deaths. The Japanese, for example, are building multistorey structures on steel springs and rubber shock absorbers to slow the side-to-side motion which often causes buildings to collapse in earthquakes. Other technologies are more simple and low cost, such as the use of deep foundations to reinforce buildings. However, because of the socio-economic circumstances of the great majority of Peruvians, particularly those in the overcrowded cities, such solutions remain outside their grasp. Their vulnerability to earthquake hazard as a result of geographical location is compounded by their inability to afford houses of a form which

Case study L *(continued)*

would go a long way towards protecting them in the event of seismic activity. In Lima alone, over three million people live in buildings that do not meet basic criteria for earthquake-resistant construction.

Figure 5.2c shows the spatial distribution of housing type in Peru, classified according to its design and its ability to withstand earth movements associated with earthquakes. The most vulnerable structures are seen to be located along the coast and in the mountainous regions. The understanding of these patterns, as shown in Figure 5.2, enables the identification of priority areas for disaster mitigation (the improvement of a community's ability to withstand the effects of environmental hazard).

Inadequate infrastructure

Whilst the urban poor may be able to secure work and shelter for themselves outside the formal provision of employment and housing by the city authorities, it is virtually impossible for them to provide for themselves the service networks which are essential to the health and the welfare of the community. Yet, budgetary allocations to the social sector, particularly during the 1980s, have decreased even further the likelihood of supplying and maintaining urban infrastructure to the urban poor. In Nairobi, for example, capital spending on water and sewerage fell from $28 per capita in 1981 to $2.50 in 1987. Social services rarely reach the urban poor, as Figure 5.3 illustrates through identifying inadequacies in the supply of water and sanitation in a number of cities in the developing world.

Ill health

It is the lack of such basic services as water supply and sanitation in the cities of the developing world which serves to keep the urban poor in ill health. Although levels of health services and expenditure in urban areas are generally higher than in rural areas, such services remain inaccessible to the urban poor through their prohibitive cost. In addition, it continues to be the diseases of poverty which affect the

Figure 5.3 Inadequacies in water supply and sanitation in selected cities of the developing world

BANGKOK   About one-third of the population has no access to public water and must obtain water from vendors. Only 2 per cent of the population is connected to a sewerage system.

CALCUTTA   Some 3 million people live in bustees and refugee settlements which lack potable water, endure serious annual flooding and have no systematic means of disposing of human wastes. Piped water is available only in the central city and parts of some other municipalities. The sewage system is limited to only a third of the area in the urban core. Poor maintenance of drains and periodic clogging of the system have made flooding an annual feature.

DAR ES SALAAM   From a survey of 660 households drawn from all income levels in 1986/7, 47 per cent had no piped water supply either inside or immediately outside their house while 32 per cent had a shared piped water supply. Of the households without piped water, 67 per cent buy water from neighbours while 26 per cent draw water from public water kiosks or standpipes. Of the sample, 7.1 per cent buy water from water sellers. Average water consumption per person is only 23.6 litres a day. For sanitation, 89 per cent had simple pit-latrines. Only 4.5 per cent had toilets connected to septic tanks or sewers. Most households have to share sanitary facilities and so overflowing latrines are a serious problem, especially in the rainy season.

JAKARTA   Less than a quarter of the population has direct connections to a piped water system; some 30 per cent depend solely on water vendors, with water costing five times that of piped water. The city has no waterborne sewage system. Septic tanks serve about 25 per cent of the population; others use pit-latrines, cesspools and ditches along the roadside. Much of the population has to use drainage canals for bathing, laundry and defecation.

SAO PAULO   In 1980, of the more than 13 million people living in the metropolitan area, 64 per cent lived in households not served by the sewage system and very little sewage was treated.

Source: Hardoy, J. E. & Satterthwaite, D. (1989) *Squatter Citizen*, London: Earthscan.

health and life expectancies of the urban poor. In several countries, there are more severely malnourished children in low income urban areas than in rural areas or higher income sectors of the city. Diseases such as diarrhoea and tuberculosis are regularly higher too. In Port-au-Prince, for example, 20 per cent of new born babies in the slum areas die before their first birthday, three times as many as in the rural areas of Haiti.

The urban environmental challenge

Clearly, poverty and poor environmental quality are inextricably related in the urban centres of the developing world. It has been seen that the urban poor, because of their low incomes, live in locations associated with substandard inherent and acquired environmental characteristics. They experience problems of the physical environment, such as flooding and landslips, and reside in close proximity to substances in the environment which are likely to be detrimental to human health. Furthermore, the urban poor experience environmental problems associated with an inadequate supply of resources essential to human health such as clean water and healthy housing conditions. Urban environmental problems in the developing world and their consequences can be considered at several different geographical scales.

Within the house and its immediate surrounds

As identified above, low-income settlements in urban areas tend to share the common characteristics of inadequate or no infrastructure and service provision, crowded conditions and locations which are unsuited to human habitation. In 1980, the World Health Organization estimated that 80 per cent of all sickness and disease worldwide was related to inadequate water (in terms of quantity and quality) and sanitation (services to collect and dispose of solid and liquid wastes). For many urban residents in cities of the developing world, the option is either to draw water from surface sources (often, in effect, open sewers) or to purchase water (of unknown quality) from vendors. It is estimated that for the urban population of the developing world as a whole, 20–30 per cent depend on water vendors for their supply. Where standpipes are provided, the quantity of water is often restricted by water being available for only a few hours a day or by the time taken in queuing for water and transporting it back to homes. In Dakar, there is on average only one standpipe for every 1,500 residents.

Clearly, the cost of water and the time taken to collect it will influence the quantity used. This, in combination with the inadequacy of urban water supplies generally, serves to explain the endemic nature of many debilitating and preventable diseases such as diarrhoea. Vulnerability to infection is also enhanced by the fact that approximately two-thirds of the urban population of the developing countries have no hygenic means of disposing of excreta or household garbage. Furthermore, the transmission of disease between individuals is often very rapid because of cramped housing conditions.

Additional environmental problems at the household level stem from the fact that, for many of the urban poor, the household is the location not only for domestic activities but also for employment. Many poor city dwellers use their homes as a workshop, as a store for goods for sale, as a shop or as a bar or café. The environmental problems related to such activities are diverse, but include the hazards to health associated with poor ventilation, inadequate light, the use of toxic or flammable chemicals and the lack of protective clothing. Household accidents account for a high proportion of disablement and serious injury in cities of the developing world, particularly amongst those groups spending large amounts of time in the household, such as women and children.

The wider neighbourhood

It has been seen that high land prices and limited availability of land in cities of the developing world force the poorest groups into the most environmentally marginal locations; to sites which are cheap because they are dangerous, but where unauthorized residents are less likely to be evicted since the land is unsuited to other forms of development. The environmental risks inherent at such sites range from implications for individual health to the large-scale loss of property, resources and even lives, such as in the event of flooding. In addition, the poor infrastructural development in the wider neighbourhood, for example the lack of storm drains, compounds the likelihood of such hazards.

The city environment

Although the developing world currently has a smaller proportion of its population resident in urban centres than has the developed world, in both absolute and relative terms the numbers are rising very rapidly. In addition, environmental problems, such as air and water pollution, operating at a city level can be considered to be more pressing in the developing world for two reasons. Firstly, industrial production has been seen to be located in a few sites within a country. Bangkok, for example, has, within the city limits, 75 per cent of Thailand's factories which deal with hazardous chemicals. Secondly, industrial development in these countries has not tended to be accompanied by effective planning or pollution control.

One effect, as seen in case study E, of the varying environmental standards and industrial pollution control which exists worldwide has been the export of hazardous wastes from those areas with strict pollution control legislation to those with little or no control. Another effect is the attraction to such locations of foreign firms who are keen to take advantage of savings on environmental controls as well as the concentration of cheap labour supplies. The city of Cubatão in Brazil has been named the 'valley of death' because of its large concentration of multinational firms and Brazilian industrial companies and the very high resultant levels of air pollution. In Cubatão, levels of respiratory infection, Infant Mortality Rates and the number of still-born and deformed babies are all substantially above those of surrounding regions. Water sources and vegetation in and around the city have also been affected; toxic wastes from these factories have contaminated the major river to the extent that fish are no longer found in it and vegetation has deteriorated from the effects of acid rain. As a result, soils become unstable and landslips occur, often leading to serious loss of life such as in February 1984 when hundreds were killed.

Citywide environmental problems also stem from activities other than industrial production. Congested road systems and poorly maintained vehicles add greatly to air pollution, as do inefficient household stoves and heaters. Case study M highlights the problem of air pollution in Mexico City. The world's most populous metropolitan area is situated in a valley surrounded by mountains, providing ideal conditions for thermal inversions in which a mass of warm air high above the city tends to trap pollutants in the cool air below. As such, Mexico City has an environment unsuited to the large concentration of industries or people which it hosts.

Case study M

Mexico's vale of tears

In March 1992, ozone levels in Mexico City had reached a record high of 398 (less than 100 is considered 'satisfactory'). The

Case study M *(continued)*

government immediately ordered more than 200 factories to cut operations by up to 75 per cent, shut schools and barred 40 per cent of cars from the streets. Within a week, the ozone index had fallen to 360 points, but a 'pollution emergency' was declared and an indefinite package of restrictions on car use and cutting factory activity by 30 per cent was announced.

Mexico City was reported to be literally choking to death; residents were complaining of sore throats, streaming eyes and burning sensations in their noses. With 15 million inhabitants, 3.5 million vehicles and 30,000 industrial employers producing 50 per cent of the country's non-oil manufacturing output, Mexico City had only 15 days in the previous year on which air quality was satisfactory.

Part of the problem is its geography. At 2,256 m, Mexico City has 23 per cent less oxygen than at sea level, so fuel burns less efficiently. Mountains surround the city on three sides and prevent pollution from dispersing. However, the main cause of ozone pollution is the motor car. Historically, transport policy in the city was geared to private motor vehicles, and petrol consumption has increased by 18 per cent since 1988. Whilst the emergency lasts, motorists are faced with restrictions on a rotating basis which could leave them without their cars for up to three days a week (including weekends). New cars must be fitted with catalytic converters and stricter annual emission tests for all cars are planned. Higher car or petrol taxes and more rigorous traffic management in favour of public transport, however, still remain outside the emergency package owing to their political sensitivity. As the city runs out of space to expand and air to breathe, the authorities will increasingly be forced to take tough decisions.

Source: Reid, M. (1992) 'Mexico's vale of tears', *Guardian*, 27 March.

Regional environmental problems

In order to support the resident populations, cities demand inputs of raw materials and goods of various natures from the surrounding region.

The larger and more prosperous the city, the greater this demand to fulfil the needs of its populace. The regional environmental impact of cities is felt in the surrounding area in terms of both the resources on which it draws and the effects of the waste and pollution which the city generates.

In the case of the urban demand for fuelwood resources, the supply necessarily comes from surrounding rural areas and, in many instances, pre-empts their use by rural residents (see Soussan in this series). Sources once available to rural inhabitants become unavailable to them as urban demand rises. This occurs through either deforestation *per se* or the commercialization of fuelwood, which makes wood a commodity to be paid for rather than a resource to be collected from communal lands. Such regional environmental effects may be felt at considerable distance from the centre of demand (the city). For example, research has shown that fuelwood for the urban population of Bangalore comes from as far away as 140 km. In Delhi, fuelwood comes by rail from Madhya Pradesh (700 km away) at a rate of 612 tons per day. In addition, the very expansion of urban settlement leads to the loss of agricultural land, including forestry resources, in the surrounding region.

Regional environmental problems associated with city-based activities are regularly linked to the inadequate provision for the safe disposal and dispersal of industrial and domestic waste. In consequence, water is often returned to sources at far lower qualities than when supplied. Regional impacts include the contamination of sources and the decline of fishing stocks. The river passing through Bolivia's largest city, La Paz, has become so polluted that horticultural production downstream has had to be curtailed. The dumping of solid wastes into water courses and soils leads to downstream health problems. For example, 120 km downstream from Bogotá, the water in the Bogotá river has faecal bacteria counts so high that it is totally unsuitable for cooking or drinking purposes. Similarly, urban industrial production may have detrimental impacts on the vegetation and crops of the surrounding region, particularly through processes of acid rain.

Other regional environmental impacts are the direct result of proximity to the urban centre. For example, the city attracts migrants from the surrounding rural areas, which has spin-offs for the rural economy in terms of the supply of labour and entrepreneurial skill. Proximity to urban centres also leads to the commercialization of land and agricultural markets in the surrounding areas. This can lead to changes in the type of crops grown and in the nature of productive activities and even to the expulsion of peasant farmers from their lands. Such processes are often inextricably linked to environmental decline in the surrounding rural areas.

Towards sustainable urban development

Conditions for change

The physical and human environments of the urban poor in cities of the developing world are amongst the most life-threatening and unhealthy living and working conditions that exist. It is the immediate adverse effects on survival for the urban poor of such basic processes as cooking, washing and working which ensure that the environmental challenges at the household level are of no less global proportions than global warming itself.

Yet it is issues of the 'global commons', such as climatic change, which have received the bulk of the attention of environmental planners in both the developing and developed nations to date. This priority is not surprising; in the developed nations, most of the regional, city, neighbourhood and housing related environmental problems outlined above have been addressed. It is the global concerns that are now likely to have the greatest impact for western economies and peoples and it is these that have also come to dominate western thought when considering the environmental problems of the developing nations. However, the environmental problems of the cities of the developing world have been seen to be much wider in scope than has been conventionally believed. For sustainable urban development, environmental planning must address the problems of the microenvironmental setting of the urban poor, those of their shelter and its immediate surrounds.

All cities are centres of both production and consumption, processes encompassing the utilization of various resources and many forms of economic activity. They are also part of the world economic system. As such and in continuity with rural livelihood systems, the urban residents of the developing world are affected by decision-making at a variety of scales. A number of conditions for sustainable urban development can therefore be identified at the international, national and local levels.

The international community has had a prominent role in the past in influencing the nature of urban growth in the developing world. In the 1950s and 1960s, economic growth through industrialization was promoted as the key to the future development of these regions. As such, it was urban centres which received the majority of overseas aid and investment during this period. Aid flowed on a project-by-project basis to various sectors of the urban environment; to industry, housing, transport and infrastructural development. In the 1960s, however, it was realized that the benefits of this 'development' were not spreading out from urban centres to smaller towns and villages as was assumed. The resultant regional disparities in income levels and opportunities were also leading to rapid rural-to-urban migration and urban growth. In the 1970s, aid was increasingly diverted to rural development projects in order to widen the benefits of development and to help to stem migration to the cities.

The nature of international aid policies remains a key factor in the prospects for future sustainable urban development. Signs of hope include the move away from narrow sectoral projects towards more integrated, multidimensional programmes for urban development. As a result, the cross-sectoral issues of food, shelter, water, land and employment (the immediate environment and development concerns of the poor) are more likely to be addressed. Currently, urban sector interests as a whole are also experiencing a renaissance within development assistance institutions.

International trading arrangements in the future will also be a key determinant of prospective sustainable urban development. For example, the moves towards continent-wide single markets and the removal of barriers to free trade will have profound implications for the location of multinational companies. This will be particularly evident across borders such as between the USA and Mexico, where there are stark differences in the urban labour costs and strength of pollution control legislation, for example. Already in Mexico, along this border, there are over 2,000 American owned factories. Mexicans are employed to assemble US raw materials to make products which are then re-imported to the USA virtually duty-free. The vast majority of these factories produce hazardous waste, employ young females and disregard health and safety standards. For example, in the town of Matamoros, people sleep, eat and work in contaminated surroundings. Forty anen-cephalic (brainless) babies have been born in the past two years to women who work in the factories located in Matamoros. In conditions of high urban unemployment and the need to service debts through foreign exchange, pressure will remain on the governments of the developing world to host foreign firms within their borders.

However, it is decision-making on behalf of national governments which in large measure will determine the conditions under which urban residents live and which will influence the future prospects for the conservation of the environment. The fundamental features of the national government and of national society (for example, the extent of inequality within the country) will be key factors in the prospects for sustainable urban development in the developing world. Authoritarian governments or the concentration of power and resources in the hands of the élite are unlikely to ensure the provision of basic needs to the urban poor.

Previous attempts by national governments in the developing world (often with the support of international institutions) to overcome regional disparities, to stem rural-to-urban migration and to address urban sectoral issues have been referred to as both highly expensive and ineffective. Such attempts have included: policies to overcome urban 'primacy' through the establishment of 'Growth Centres' in less developed regions; the introduction of rural minimum wages to improve the viability of non-agricultural employment opportunities in the rural areas; and programmes of squatter settlement removal. In all, there has been an insufficient environmental emphasis within urban planning.

However, whilst national governments can lay down a broad range of policies in such areas as economic development and infrastructural investment and can legislate the basis upon which orderly government can proceed, it is increasingly realized that it is local authorities and communities themselves that are best able to set priorities for and implement projects to affect the nature of much urban development. In order for this to be done, there is a need for the decentralization of power and resources from central government, the mobilization of municipal revenue through local sources with the active participation of private sector and community organizations, and an emphasis on 'enabling' strategies targeted on the weakest sections of society.

The WCED stated that, beyond the development of a broad urban strategy, the primary role of central governments should be to strengthen the capacity of local governments to find and carry through effective solutions to local urban problems and stimulate local opportunities. To become such 'agents of development', local authorities need enhanced political, institutional and financial capacity. In many developing countries at present, the institutional and legal structures of local government are inadequate to effect such changes.

It is now realized that there is a substantial human resource amongst the urban poor in the developing world which could be mobilized to achieve the objectives of sustainable urban development. For example, the informal sector economy provides many of the cheap goods and services essential to city economies, business and consumers (see Drakakis-Smith in this series). Much of the building and upgrading in the city is also done outside official plans and by informal sector builders. Such activities provide important sources of income particularly for low-skilled labour, are flexible in responding to local needs, and are not energy, capital or technology-intensive. They do, however, perform vital functions in urban development. Local authorities, governments and development assistance agencies must give more support to this informal sector for sustainable development of the cities of the developing world.

Characteristics of success

Human settlements in the developing world exhibit substantial diversity at the macro scale. For example, there are 18 'mega-cities' of over ten million inhabitants in Latin America and Asia, whilst less than 10 per cent of Ethiopia's population are resident in towns and cities. However, it has been seen that low-income settlements throughout the cities of the developing world share the common characteristics of cramped, unhealthy housing, insecurity of tenure, a lack of basic services and low incomes.

A number of common characteristics can also be identified for sustainable urban development, based on recent successful experience. The lessons to be learned include the following:

1 Housing is also a people's problem;
2 The need for building communities;
3 The need for organizing the community;
4 The importance of outsiders;
5 The importance of external funding.

The first prerequisite for sustainable urban development is to recognize that housing is not only a problem for central government, local authorities and the private sector but also a concern for communities themselves. Given the chance, poor people can hold the key to the solution of their own housing problem. Urban development projects which are sustainable have shown a variety of ways in which local communities can be supported in improving their housing. These include legislative reforms and the provision of basic infrastructure.

The second and third lessons show that improving human settlements should involve more than change in the physical structures of housing. Long-term sustainability is more likely to be achieved through 'building the community'; through assisting communities to become socially organized in the course of a physical building programme. In order for community development to occur, poor people themselves must be actors in the process, must develop a social conscience and should represent the values of the wider community of which they are a part. Methods for organizing a community to improve housing conditions are varied. Sustainable projects have used methodologies such as mobile training teams, political party frameworks, women's organizations and groups based on a number of houses or streets. All have shared the common approach of 'learning-by-doing'; methods for organization were flexible and were adapted on the basis of ongoing experience and evaluation of the project.

The fourth prerequisite for sustainable urban development is that projects should have external assistance in terms of support from groups such as NGOs. Such 'outsiders' have an important role in enabling communities to improve their own environments through giving support and advice in technical, legal, accountancy and social fields for example. NGOs are particularly suited to a role as 'enablers' of the community but also as mediators with central government.

External funding is the final prerequisite which has been seen to be critical to the success of sustainable urban development projects. Physical constructions and development work in a community require financial resources which are often unavailable within the community itself or through government sources. External sources, critically foreign aid, are therefore very important particularly in the early stages of a project. In addition, the enabling activities of NGO staff are also clearly dependent on funding from outside the project. Case study N illustrates the characteristics of a sanitation project in a squatter settlement of Karachi which were central to its sustainability.

Case study N

The Orangi Pilot Project, Karachi, Pakistan

Orangi is the largest squatter settlement in Karachi. Since 1980, approximately 50 per cent of households in this community have

---

Case study N *(continued)*

been part of the Orangi Pilot Project (OPP), financed by the Bank of Credit and Commerce International, to improve conditions of sanitation. Services for the disposal of excreta and waste water had been non-existent in the area prior to this date.

Finance for the project had to be found largely from within the community itself. OPP was to provide mainly research and extension services and limited capital inputs. Since Orangi is only one of 362 squatter settlements in Karachi alone, the prospects of international finance were unlikely and would carry the additional problem of repayment. Local authority services also remained outside the community's reach in terms of expense. The project therefore focused on finding out what methods for waste disposal were currently being used by the community, selecting the most desirable and building on these to achieve a low cost method of sanitation within the community.

An underground system of sewerage lines was chosen. Community organizations were created, based on lanes encompassing 20 or 30 houses. Paid employees of OPP held meetings with residents in order to explain the programme and its economic and health benefits. If all of the residents of each 'lane' agreed to participate, they would receive the support of OPP to construct sewerage lines in their area. Each participating unit then elected a 'lane manager' who acted on behalf of the residents in subsequent dealings with OPP. These managers were also responsible for the implementation of the project (including handling of the money collected from the people).

OPP staff continue to be involved in undertaking surveys, giving technical advice, organizing extension activities, overseeing construction and providing capital expenditure. By 1985, over 1,500 lanes had built their sewerage system and 137 secondary drains (linking local drains into a wider community network) had been constructed. The people had invested over US$1.5 million in this effort and OPP US$94,000. The cost to the local authority of doing this work would have been over US$8 million for which the local community would have been charged.

The OPP was successful in that it has provided sanitation to over

Case study N *(continued)*

> 43,000 housing units at a development cost to the user of one-sixth of what it would have been if such a service had been provided by the Karachi Municipal Corporation. In addition, there are no problems of collecting charges or recovering loans for the local authority and maintenance is undertaken by the residents themselves.
>
> Major environmental changes have occurred in the Orangi settlement; human health has improved, people are upgrading their houses and the value of these has gone up. The experience of community participation in a project having clear benefits to individual households has led to improved social harmony in the area which is likely to encourage the future sustainable development of these urban settlements.

Conclusion

In continuity with the lessons learned about promoting sustainable rural livelihoods, urban development in the future must focus on the welfare needs of the poorest sectors of the towns and cities of the developing world in order to be sustainable. The urban environments of the poor are extremely hazardous to human health and the people themselves represent a substantial resource for the improvement of these environments. Enabling poor communities to take control of their own development is the starting point for achieving levels of urban development and environmental change which are less likely to be met by international and/or government finances. Environment and development concerns amongst the majority of urban residents in the developing countries are explicitly interdependent. Unemployment and underemployment are closely related to poverty and, in turn, to hazardous and deteriorating living and working conditions. Future sustainable urban development must necessarily address these issues as being integrated rather than via narrow sectoral programmes.

The major constraints on and necessary conditions for sustainable urban development have been identified at a variety of levels from community organization to international political and economic activities. Prospects for sustainable urban development are also tied closely to those of securing sustainable rural livelihoods. Rural-to-urban migration remains an important force in urban growth. Policy and practice in such areas as economic support for agricultural produce and urban food pricing will therefore have an important effect on the movement of people from rural areas to the towns and cities. The challenges and opportunities of sustainable development lie in providing security for individuals in meeting their basic needs; only then will they be able to take a long-term view of development and the environment.

Key ideas

1 Patterns and processes of urban development in the developing world are without historical precedent.
2 The majority of the urban poor in the developing world have low incomes, inferior housing, a lack of basic infrastructural services, are highly vulnerable to environmental hazards and suffer from ill health.
3 Urban environmental problems in the developing world and their consequences can be considered at a variety of scales.
4 Action for sustainable urban development needs to be taken at all levels, but local authorities and communities themselves may be best able to set priorities for and implement projects.
5 Enabling poor communities to participate in the upgrading of their own settlements is likely to be both cost effective and sustainable.

6
Sustainable development in the developing world: an assessment

Fundamental dilemmas

> Every human society exhibits a tension between a desire to exploit and an obligation to protect. Some turn to the Gods to help them, some to more natural orders, others to science, technology and managerial ingenuity.
>
> (O'Riordan 1990)

Sustainable development is the term currently used to refer to the challenge facing contemporary human society of reconciling future progress (development) with the protection of the environment. The concept of sustainable development emerged in the 1980s in recognition of the realities of the operation of human societies, their interactions across the globe and the nature of the environment in which people now live. Past patterns and processes of development have led to the current situation in which fulfilling the needs of residents in any part of the world in future are influenced by the actions of many others outside the particular location under question. Furthermore, the environmental concerns of individuals and the global community as a whole are intimately linked to these development challenges. There is now a recognition that human activities are impacting on the environment at a global level which has no known historical precedent. This reality demands that all citizens of the world have an obligation to take action to protect resources which may seem far removed from the operation of the immediate society in which they live.

It is these realities of the environment today and the functioning of contemporary societies which make the challenge of reconciling the tension between the desire to exploit and the obligation to protect (sustainable development) substantially different to that within earlier societies. It has been seen that human societies in history were not dependent on such collective actions to the same degree as contemporary society. At lower levels of population and technology in particular, their resultant impact on the environment tended to be smaller and more localized in extent. Under such circumstances, recourse to spiritual or technical solutions in the protection of resources for future generations were often effective ways of ensuring sustainable futures for their populations.

However, there is more uncertainty as to the most appropriate means through which human society today can ensure that the ability of future generations to fulfil their own needs are not compromised by contemporary desires to exploit. The harmful effects of existing technology are currently outpacing the development of new ones which are needed to protect the environment through resource substitution, waste minimization and recycling. In addition, the existing dominance of scientific values and ways of thinking within societies across the globe today have reduced the flexibility and capacity for environmental protection through alternative technologies, cultural structures or views of the environment.

A critique

The WCED report is accepted widely as having been very influential in bringing the concept of sustainable development into the popular conscience, particularly in the developed world. It has also been central in the subsequent debate regarding the recommendations made for the future exploitation and protection of the resources of the world. However, the concept of sustainable development has also been seen to have roots which extend back into the history of the theory and practice of both 'development' and 'environmentalism'. There remain today contrasting approaches to development and the environment which have been important in putting forward a critique of the concept of sustainable development in operation generally and the recommendations of the WCED in particular. These can be termed the 'ecology-centred', 'market-based' and 'neo-Marxist' approaches.

Although each of these three major stances on the environment and development puts forward distinct views of sustainable development, owing to the differing 'starting points' from which they emerge, it is apparent that all view sustainable development as inherently desirable and a policy objective which should be striven for. One commentator suggests that this is a realistic assessment of the current environment and development challenges facing human society: 'new insights into physical and social phenomena force one to concur with the operational conclusions of the sustainable development platform almost regardless of one's fundamental ethical persuasions and priorities.'

The starting point for proponents of the ecology-centred approach is that economic growth and environmental conservation are contradictory. They are anti-growth and advocate a steady-state economy and the distribution of resources more equitably. This approach therefore has a conception of sustainable development which is in opposition to that of the WCED which believes that the technical solutions to environmental degradation can be found through economic growth. The two are, however, in agreement concerning the role of local participation and action as the practical basis for tackling many environment and development problems in the developing world.

The market-based approach to development and the environment starts from the principle that growth and technical advancement in a free-market economy are the keys to sustainable development in the future. Success is seen to depend on sufficient political will and the ability to place a market value on the environment and the economic functions that it enables. Proponents of this approach therefore tend to show greater support for the recommendations of the WCED than those of the ecology-centred approach. It is suggested that, through modification of established economic formulae and techniques such as cost-benefit analysis, it is possible to put a correct value on the environment and ensure that the next generations inherit environmental assets which are not less than (although perhaps different from) those which the current population enjoys.

The starting point for the neo-Marxist approach is the inequality which exists between major regions of the world. Proponents of this approach suggest that sustainable development is not achievable within the existing world system. They highlight the political and economic processes which link people and places and which serve to keep some areas underdeveloped whilst simultaneously enabling others to exploit these regions in the course of their own development. They suggest that the recommendations for action made by the WCED are desirable but unobtainable outside a fundamental restructuring of the global economy.

Optimism and flexibility

This book has presented a number of insights into the challenges, opportunities and progress made with regard to sustainable development in practice in the developing world. The achievements made have been secured without revolutionary political and economic change in the world system (although many national frameworks in Eastern Europe and the former USSR have undergone fundamental restructuring). These achievements have, however, involved a reassessment on behalf of individuals, nations, NGOs and international institutions of the constraints and opportunities of development and the environment (both natural and structural) and of the criteria for success in the exploitation and protection of the resources of the world.

Capitalism is the framework within which action for sustainable development has to be taken, since currently there is no alternative. The progress made towards sustainable development as seen in this book is indicative of the flexibility of the capitalist system to adapt to the challenge of both economic and environmental sustainability. However, the shortfalls which have also been identified are confirmation that continued progress depends on 'political will and government intervention into a dynamic economic system whose overriding motor drive is to maximize profits' (Smith 1991). Ensuring that governments do indeed take the required and appropriate actions for sustainable development demands continued public pressure from individuals, NGOs and representatives of business, commerce and industry. As Timberlake (1991) suggests, it is people who *do* development, not governments, and therefore sustainable development is ultimately a local activity.

Such pressure depends in turn on individual understanding of the challenges and opportunities of sustainable development. Although the power of individuals to respond and take action on the basis of this understanding varies, as Chambers (1983) has noted, all are to some degree capable of changing what they do even in small ways. This requires a personal reassessment of needs and wants, of commitment to the wider community and of obligations to future generations.

The WCED report has been important in giving direction concerning the changes in thinking and action required on behalf of individuals for sustainable development in the future. Continued economic growth is required but in new ways which ensure a reasonable and equitable level of economic well-being for all citizens of the global community. Increasing the material wealth of those in poverty is the 'quantitative' dimension of sustainable development. However, economic well-being itself must include non-economic values such as liberty, dignity and spiritual well-being. These are the criteria for successful sustainable development which have been overlooked within existing processes of development and have resulted in the patterns of poverty and environmental deterioration described in this book. Progress towards such 'qualitative' aspects of sustainable development is hard to assess; they are long term and multi-faceted, but nevertheless essential for ensuring the ecological, social and cultural potential for supporting economic activity in the future.

The quantitative and qualitative dimensions of sustainable development are inseparable and mutually reinforcing. The examples in this book of successful sustainable development projects confirmed the positive synergism to be gained from prioritizing local knowledge and needs in programmes which enabled communities to improve their own welfare and that of the environment. The outcome was seen to be greater than the sum of the parts; benefits were gained from addressing the environment and development together which have not been achieved through separate programmes. For example, people gained security against becoming poorer within such projects and, in so doing, achieved the power to participate in further change. It is these characteristics of success which give optimism for future sustainable development.

However, there can be no single or neatly defined prescription for change. It is not possible, for example, to predict what the likely interests of future generations will be, how much technological progress will be made or the precise outcome of global warming. However, these are not justifications for inaction today. The obligation of the current generation is both to exploit and to protect the resources of the world in ways which do not preclude options for such actions tomorrow.

Key ideas

1 All societies face a number of dilemmas in resource use. These include: the tension between a desire to exploit (now) and the obligation to protect (for the future); the distinction between basic and extravagant needs; and a commitment to both self and the

community. In the past, human societies have made recourse to various strategies for reconciling these dilemmas.

2 The concept of sustainable development encapsulates these same challenges for contemporary society.

3 Criticisms of the concept of sustainable development generally and the WCED specifically have come from three major stances on development and the environment.

4 The progress and limitations of sustainable development in practice have confirmed both the flexibility of the capitalist system to respond to the economic and ecological challenges and the need for continued pressure for change.

5 There is no blueprint for sustainable development in the future. It requires flexibility in terms of action and criteria for success, accommodating both quantitative and qualitative change.

Review questions and further reading

1 What is sustainable development?

Review questions

1 When and why did the concept of sustainable development take shape?
2 How have ideas about the meaning of 'development' changed in the 1960s, 1970s and 1980s?
3 Consider the ways in which global deforestation can be viewed as both a major environmental and development problem.

Further reading

Adams, W. M. (1990) *Green Development: Environment and Sustainability in the Third World*, London: Routledge.
Court, T. de la (1990) *Beyond Brundtland: Green Development in the 1990s*, London: Zed Books.
Redclift, M. R. (1984) *Development and the Environmental Crisis: Red or Green alternatives*, London: Methuen.
Redclift, M. R. (1987) *Sustainable Development: Exploring the Contradictions*, London: Methuen.
World Commission on Environment and Development (1987) *Our Common Future*, Oxford: Oxford University Press.

2 The challenge of sustainable development

Review questions

1 Identify the challenges to sustainable development presented by the fact that, in large measure, 'wealth determines health'.
2 Select a 'supranational' environmental issue and identify its major causes and consequences. In what ways can it be considered a problem for the global community?

Further reading

Jackson, B. (1990) *Poverty and the Planet: A Question of Survival*, London: Penguin.
Leggett, J. (ed.) (1990) *Global Warming: The Greenpeace Report*, Oxford: Oxford University Press.
Myers, N. and Myers, D. (1982) 'Increasing awareness of the supranational nature of emerging environmental issues', *Ambio* 11 (4): 195–201.
Timberlake, L. and Thomas, L. (1990) *When the Bough Breaks: Our Children, Our Environment*, London: Earthscan.
Todaro, M. P. (1989) *Economic Development in the Third World*, London: Longman.
World Commission on Environment and Development (1987) *Our Common Future*, Oxford: Oxford University Press.

3 Action towards sustainable development

Review questions

1 To what extent do you feel that the World Bank is committed to sustainable development?
2 Consider the arguments for and against free-trade and assess the likely impacts on the environment.
3 What do you think the reaction of different sections of the Dutch population may have been to their government's national environmental policy plan?
4 Compare the role of national governments and Non-Governmental Organizations in future sustainable development.
5 Compile a list of potential factors influencing the decisions of an industrialized country to export hazardous waste and those of a developing country to receive these pollutants.

Further reading

Conroy, C. and Litvinoff, M. (1988) *The Greening of Aid: Sustainable Livelihoods in Practice*, London: Earthscan.

Hayter, T. (1989) *Exploited Earth: Britain's Aid and the Environment*, London: Earthscan.
Marray, M. (1991) 'Natural forgiveness', *Geographical Magazine*, December, 18–22.
Rich, B. M. (1989) 'The greening of the development banks; rhetoric and reality', *Ecologist* 19 (2): 44–52.
Starke, L. (1990) *Signs of Hope: Working towards Our Common Future*, Oxford: Oxford University Press.
World Commission on Environment and Development (1987) *Our Common Future*, Oxford: Oxford University Press.

4 Sustainable rural livelihoods

Review questions

1 Summarize the characteristics of the majority of farmers in the developing world today.
2 Identify some of the possible barriers to the 'farmer first' approach to research and development.
3 With reference to Figure 4.1, assess the impact at various levels in the world agroecosystem of crop failure owing to drought for a large number of farmers in Africa, for example.

Further reading

Chambers, R. (1983) *Rural Development: Putting the Last First*, London: Longman.
Conroy, C. and Litvinoff, M. (1988) *The Greening of Aid: Sustainable Livelihoods in Practice*, London: Earthscan.
Dixon, C. (1991) *Rural Development in the Third World*, London: Routledge.
Leonard, H. J. (1989) *Environment and the Poor: Development Strategies for a Common Agenda*, Oxford: Transaction Books.
Momsen, J. H. (1991) *Women and Development in the Third World*, London: Routledge.
Rodda, A. (1991) *Women and the Environment*, London: Zed Books.
Scott, E. P. (ed.) (1984) *Life Before the Drought*, London: Allen & Unwin.

5 Sustainable urban livelihoods

Review questions

1 How have the patterns and processes of urban development in the developing world differed from those in the developed world?
2 With reference to the cities of the developing world, illustrate the meaning of the term 'pollution of poverty'.

3 Collect further evidence for the suggestion that communities themselves can help to upgrade their own standards of housing. Are these likely to be sustainable?

Further reading

Conroy, C. and Litvinoff, M. (1988) *The Greening of Aid: Sustainable Livelihoods in Practice*, London: Earthscan.
Cuny, F. C. (1983) *Disasters and Development*, Oxford: Oxford University Press.
Drakakis-Smith, D. (1987) *The Third World City*, London: Routledge.
Hardoy, J. E. and Satterthwaite, D. (1989) *Squatter Citizen*, London: Earthscan.
Hardoy, J. E., Cairncross, S. and Satterthwaite, D. (eds) (1990) *The Poor Die Young: Housing and Health in Third World Cities*, London: Earthscan.

6 Sustainable development in the developing world: an assessment

Review questions

1 Which of the three major stances on environment and development high-lighted in this chapter do you consider presents the most realistic assessment of the prospects for sustainable development?
2 For your local area, identify possible evidence of a reassessment of develop-ment and the environment which has occurred in sections of the community, such as individuals, business and industry.

Further reading

O'Riordan, T. (1990) 'Major projects and the environment', *Geographical Journal* 156 (2): 141–8.
Pearce, D. *et al* (1989) *Blueprint for a Green Economy*, London: Earthscan.
Smith, P. M. and Warr, K. (ed) (1991) *Global Environmental Issues*, London: Hodder & Stoughton.
Timberlake, L. and Holmberg, J. (1991) *Defending the Future: A Guide to Sustainable Development*, London: Earthscan.

Index